"When a book arrives at just the right time — it demands attention. Kate Burton cares about people and her observation and sensitive record of the hectic lifestyle so many of us lead means this outstanding book will resonate. With practical ideas and new thinking, you are inspired to take action to change your relationship with work and create a sustainable mix with the life you must own. This presents us the opportunity to 'glow' with energy at work, at home and at play. We'd be mad not to take it!"

Farren Drury MBE, Director LIW

"Live Life, Love Work really resonated with me. It's precisely the type of themes explored in this book that have made a difference in my career as an Olympic rower."

Steve Williams OBE, British Olympic Gold Medallist and Leadership Team Developer

"Kate Burton, author of the acclaimed *NLP for Dummies*, focuses this time on the importance of talent and values when building careers — so much more critical than just the right CV."

Anne Watson, International Headhunter and Business Book Author

"If you need the inspiration to change your life for the better this is the book for you. Kate Burton invites us to take real steps towards our dreams and lights the path with excellent exercises and realistic advice from people who have made it happen for them, Now it's your turn!"

Rosie Miller, International Executive Coach

To Bob

for providing the rock solid foundation of love

LIVE LIFE
LOVE WORK

Kate Burton

CAPSTONE
be inspired! ™

This edition first published 2010

© 2010 Kate Burton

Registered office

Capstone Publishing Ltd. (A Wiley Company), The Atrium, Southern Gate, Chichester, West Sussex, PO19 8SQ, United Kingdom

For details of our global editorial offices, for customer services and for information about how to apply for permission to reuse the copyright material in this book please see our website at www.wiley.com.

Library of Congress Cataloguing-in-Publication Data

9781907312021

A catalogue record for this book is available from the British Library.

Set in 11.5 on 14pt Adobe Caslon Pro-Regular by aptara

Printed by TJ International Ltd. Padstow, Cornwall

CONTENTS

Kate Burton is a well-respected, fully qualified international coach who challenges her clients to transform their personal effectiveness, leadership style and performance.

Her clients number many senior executives with a hearty appetite for development; people who value success, expect a high quality of life and measure the impact of coaching on their bottom line performance. Kate is a master practitioner in Neuro-Linguistic Programming and a full member of the International Coach Federation with PCC accreditation.

Also by Kate Burton:

with Brinley Platts

Building Self Confidence for Dummies

with Romilla Ready

Neuro-Linguistic Programming for Dummies

Neuro-Linguistic Programming Workbook for Dummies

Personal Development All in One

Job Hunting And Career Change All in One

AUTHOR'S NOTE

The stories featured in *Live Life Love Work* are based on real people. In some cases, actual names are used, with permission. In others, names are changed and composite characters have been created. It's my hope that, through others' stories, you will gain insights into creating the most healthy and productive life that you wish for.

ACKNOWLEDGEMENTS

I would like to thank everyone who has seen this project safely on its journey, including those who freely shared their stories and experiences, and clients who allowed me to experiment with the ideas, as well as friends who provided quiet writing time, space and wonderful perspectives. My special appreciation goes to my commissioning editor, Emma Swaisland, at Capstone for her commitment to this work as well as Grace O'Byrne, Jenny Ng and Sarah Sutton for their professional expertise.

INTRODUCTION

The Nature of Energy

Time and Priorities

Taking Action

The Key Principles to Live Life, Love Work

This is a book for real people with real lives: people like you and me who need to earn a living and also want a great life. It came about because I dreamt of escaping to a beach house where life would be idyllic, and then woke up to see that wouldn't be so much fun. The escape plan missed the point.

What became more attractive was to live a rich and full life that included the mental challenge of interesting work, the friendship of colleagues, the satisfaction of making a contribution to others' lives. At the same time, to live this life and love work in a calm, healthy and sustainable way, having fun and spending time with those who matter.

Other people I meet want a similarly rich life and work that brings a sense of fun, adventure and being alive. They want to use their special talents and make a difference through what they do. Work gives us a huge sense of our identity, and quitting early often proves to be a disappointment. As David, a colleague, said: 'I came to a point where I realised that I needed work more than work needed me.' Good work, when we find it, yields wealth beyond financial rewards.

The heart of this book explores the question: 'How do we stay sane, healthy and optimistic without chucking in our jobs, selling up our businesses, leaving friends and family to head to the beach, the mountains or the other side of the world?' The answers are not always simple, nor do they lie in a one-off choice. Instead, getting to a place of satisfaction with life is a continual process of gathering information, making decisions, choosing a direction to follow and taking action as the world around us changes. As we sift through opportunities and blend the special elements of the mix that are best for us, then we own our lives.

My intent, as you travel through these pages with me, is that you gain fresh insights that create the difference for you between making a living and having a life; between simply existing or living life to the full. You will find these insights in various ways:

» By hearing others' stories
» Exploring practical exercises for yourself
» Giving yourself space to ponder the ideas

ultimately, to shift from places where you feel stuck to opening up choices and new possibilities involves taking action. The insights remain in your head as pure ideas until you make the first step.

THE NATURE OF ENERGY

The journey we'll be taking together focuses on harnessing your personal energy as a guide to getting the best experience and in Chapter 1, I invite you to check in with an Energy Audit to identify areas where your energy is blocked. This notion of energy is not something tangible that you can see or touch like oil, coal or an electric wire. Yet when you pay attention, you know when you have energy and when it's missing; you feel the effect.

Energy is most likely to be experienced as a feeling. The positive stands out in contrast to the negative: excited rather than disillusioned; cheerful and happy-go-lucky rather than put upon and stressed. It's the difference between feeling light and optimistic compared to weary and downhearted; between feeling valued or worthless; between feeling needed and involved or an outsider. Good energy that flows is about that sense of wellbeing and contentment that makes activity almost effortless and free-flowing.

Specifically, you'll begin to notice your sense of wellbeing at the physical, mental, emotional, and purposeful or spiritual levels.

Physical energy — is about nurturing a healthy body, which we explore in Chapter Two.

Mental energy — is about following your intellectual powers and talents, which we explore in Chapter Three.

Emotional energy — is about tuning into feelings and taking control of them, which we explore in Chapter Four.

Purposeful energy — is about developing a clear sense of direction according to your passion and values, which we explore in Chapter Five.

TIME AND PRIORITIES

One life is not long enough for all the things we want to do. Energy is inextricably linked with time and setting priorities about how we spend it. Who ever has enough time? Getting more time is impossible – there are only ever 24 hours in a day, 168 hours in a week. Our thinking about time shifts when we allow ourselves the space to listen to our energy and then allocate time on the truly important things, saying 'no' to what no longer works, and a resounding 'yes' to what we really want.

While time management is important to provide structure and focus in busy lives, it can also become the logical activity that backfires on us, encouraging us to pack more and more content into lives that are already bursting at the seams, building ever-longer 'to do' lists. The important thing is not to attempt to manage time by being super efficient, but to allocate your time to those things that give you energy, rather than draining it, and trusting that setting the priorities in this way will take you in the best direction.

For example, if you were looking for a new job, the details on paper can appear idyllic, but to actually fall in love with that work involves allowing yourself to listen to your heart as well as your head. It's in this space of awareness that great things happen.

TAKING ACTION

Have you heard the story about the three frogs sitting on a lily pad and one decides to jump? The question is: 'How many are then left?' The answer is 'All three because none of them moved.' The moral of the tale is that making a decision is useless without taking action.

In Chapter Six, we'll be looking at taking action for change. Change is a process that requires you to:

» Set the intention about what you want. This is where goal setting around priorities comes in.
» Pay attention to shifting your energy towards that outcome. Here, planning your time and gathering your resources is important.

» Make a personal commitment to embrace change. This entails getting in touch with your true motivation.

» Take the first step. Yippee, then the action begins.

Aiming for the whole self

Our working lives are predicted to be longer than we expected a few years back. A UK survey conducted by the Chartered Institute of Personnel Development (CIPD) in 2009 showed that 70% of those aged 55 and above anticipate to be working beyond state pension age compared to 40% two years ago. Younger people may not have thought decades ahead, but the chances are they will have inadequate funding for a comfortable early retirement.

Workers everywhere are likely to need increased levels of motivation and job satisfaction to sustain them for longer. Work brings with it the tension between opposing demands on us; this is a natural part of life. In the ancient Eastern philosophies, the principles of 'yin' and 'yang' suggest that the whole is always experienced as two parts that naturally stretch and pull each other: night and day, masculine and feminine, pleasure and pain, work and play. This tension keeps us growing and learning and the dynamic of life alive.

In the western psychoanalytic traditions, Freud and Jung suggested that splitting the world is not successful. When you split off part of yourself, it doesn't lead to happiness. You can only be happy when you accept the shadow side, the part that keeps you awake at night and anxious. Then everything is in the open and you have nothing left to fear.

Just as Freud and Jung's work was all about integration of the whole person, so this book is about being the whole of yourself, firing on all cylinders and moving in the right direction for you. In life, we split ourselves into many different roles and 'parts'. There will be differences that lead to conflict between them, and the more we recognise that, go with it and stop trying to control it, then the easier life becomes.

There are clues to our motivation from our past. When my maternal grandmother brought up a family of five children in the 1920s, she had with no state support after her first husband was killed in the First World War. She worked late into the night making children's clothes that paid the rent and bought food.

When I set up my own business after the birth of my first child, I also worked at home late into the night while the baby slept and, like my grandmother, was paid only for the work I delivered. Over the years, I switched and refined my work from freelance writing to marketing programmes, to soft skills training, communications consultancy and then professional coaching.

The original interviewing and writing tasks that I performed have evolved into doing work that I truly love, listening to people and helping to shape their lives and work. This work is so much a part of my identity that I can't imagine not doing it in some shape or form.

From tension to strategies

If you've picked up this book, then I'm assuming that you too want work that works for you. You may identify with some of the stories that I will tell about the real physical, mental and emotional pressures that people face.

> *Tessa advises organisations about stress management. As her own business became busier and more successful, she found herself taking on a diary packed with commitments. One day, her body shut down with overload just as if her own laptop had run out of disk space. 'I crashed and didn't see it coming.'*
>
> *With pressure pushed down the line from the Minister of his government department, James felt bullied by his boss making unreasonable demands on his time. Working crazy hours on constantly changing projects led to rows at home, and he walked away from his wife and family into the arms of a sympathetic colleague. 'I just want to leave the job and move away.'*

Brenda is passionate about her role as Chief Executive of a Charitable Foundation. However, her husband's progressive illness means he will soon be incapable of holding down his job, and her elderly parents need care too. Each night Brenda comes home from work, opens a bottle of wine: 'I need to cheer myself up, and then feel so bad about it later.'

Just as life is not perfect, stories are not black and white. People have the natural resilience to find new strategies when life gets tough.

Amanda, a feisty, well-educated mother of three sons, runs a small consultancy yet allocates time to manage the costume production for the juniors' school play each year. Each evening, she blocks out two hours for family time when the boys get her undivided attention. 'I want to be there for my boys and give them each time for a proper conversation.'

Edwin runs a software sales team. When he encounters the person ready to dump their troubles on him, he diverts them to a similar negative soul with a graceful introduction. 'I keep away from anybody or anything that leaves me exhausted,' he says. By tuning into the effect certain people have on him, he sustains his natural enthusiasm and energy.

Fran's learnt about creating her own calm space within work conflicts. Her reputation as a tough Human Resources Director has been built up over twenty years of leading negotiations with unions. She has the job of delivering news of further cuts and redundancies. Few people know that she endured an abusive marriage for many years. 'It was my yoga and meditation classes that brought me through this and gave me courage to make different choices.'

Today, there is no set formula for a perfect working life, but a menu of options to choose from at different transition points. On a day-to-day basis, our 'work' begins with a series of tangible tasks, the things that we do for which we are rewarded. When we look at our work in the longer context of a career or a satisfying life, we move away from thinking of the immediate tasks, those items on the 'to do' lists, to consider adjusting the work we do so that it fits with our values, passion and purpose.

From these pages, you'll take away an increased sense of what is possible for you and the ability to learn from others who've been on a similar journey. From other people's stories, I hope that you will begin to write your own story, exactly the way you want it to be. Have fun.

THE KEY PRINCIPLES TO
LIVE LIFE, LOVE WORK

» **Physical energy**. Begin with looking after your health
and maximising your physical wellbeing. This is the
foundation from which everything else flows.

» **Mental energy**. Develop your intellectual and mental
resilience, harnessing your talents and allowing space for
your playful creativity to emerge.

» **Emotional energy**. Get your emotions in check. Notice
your moods and what triggers an upset for you so that
you steer smoothly through the peaks and troughs.

» **Purposeful energy**. Connect with your values, beliefs
and sense of purpose. Knowing what's most important
to you enables you to follow the direction that is
right for you and where you can make the greatest
contribution to the world.

» **Be brave and take action**. Make changes and take
risks, starting with the first step – that one you're most
reluctant to take.

From the stories I've heard, I've extracted these core principles to loving our lives which entail reclaiming our energy.
Each of these principles is explored in depth in the following chapters.

CHAPTER 1

SETTING OFF

We often recognise what is 'right' in our lives only when we experience what is going 'wrong'. It can be a painful experience to notice that we are stuck, that some intangible 'thing' is missing or blocking our way, that something is not fitting just right. This is a valuable warning signal that our energy is not flowing and therefore we are not going to operate at our best or be at our happiest.

This chapter will help identify challenges that we face where our energy could be stuck or blocked – and ways to free it up. Ultimately, the aim is to remain calm, strong and at one with ourselves as we travel rather than be shattered into thousands of small pieces under pressure; to take ourselves to an edge that allows us to stretch and grow by following what is right for us as individuals.

Everybody I interviewed for this book had their own good times/bad times tales to share. In the good times they felt integrated and whole; in the bad times they felt stressed and shattered. Right now you may be experiencing either extreme.

For many people, intense back-to-back working with long hours and no recovery time is their normal routine. They become like the proverbial boiled frogs, those little creatures popped into a pan of cold water. The heat builds up and up, and they don't notice the gradual increase until it is too late and they're cooked. Each year these people work that bit harder and longer until the work itself loses its excitement and the rest of life gets seriously infected. Often a crisis stops them in their tracks.

Remember that we are offered more opportunities based on our track record and thus set the pattern for our lives. If we want to create a new pattern, we have to make clear to others the new direction that we are following, rather than accepting more of the same.

Instead of being a boiled frog, you can choose to be the hero of your own life.

QUIT BATTLING AND SEIZE THE MOMENT

All of us will hit turning points where we have a strong sense that things aren't working or where they can be better, and those points come at different times in our lives. Clearly age has an impact. As I get older, I have learnt from experience and been through the personal development that enables me to recognise that I want more from my work than money; I want a healthy, sustainable quality of life.

With age we also recognise that life is actually a very short time span. Even if we live to be 110, that wouldn't be sufficient. One life is never going to be long enough to visit all the awesome places and do all the things we could do.

Each generation learns from the previous one what it wants and doesn't. My own daughter, recently graduated from university, has a job in Europe that enables her to work with an international set of colleagues, build on her language skills, and be socially responsible. She knows she doesn't want the kind of work that chains her like a young puppy to the same desk and computer in a faceless office.

Today's young professionals are well travelled and confident. They don't want to become part of what David Bolchover calls a generation of *The Living Dead* in his book of the same name, where 'presenteeism' is the name of the game and you are measured by hours at your desk rather than your contribution. What's harder to work out is what they do want and that may only become clear as they travel.

Mapping your hero's journey

As we mature, we discover that life offers us many different roles to play at any one time – lover, spouse, friend, student, employee or business owner, product developer, computer whizz, artist, reader, writer, fundraiser, gardener, adventurer, homemaker, fighter pilot, healer, parent or child – plus many more. One life comprises a unique combination of roles which don't always fit together smoothly.

Our navigation through life and work can be likened to the stages in Joseph Campbell's famous 'hero's journey' from his classic book *The Hero with a Thousand Faces*. Back in the 1940s, Campbell pointed to certain consistent patterns and structures in myths and stories which contained a central character – the hero, along with mentors, allies and villains.

Campbell's work was subsequently developed by Christopher Vogler in his book, *The Writer's Journey*, into a 12-stage framework which is often adopted to guide the development of fiction and film scripts. Most classic films and tales from *The Wizard of Oz* and *Gladiator* to Homer's *Odyssey* or Tolkein's *Lord of the Rings* can be mapped onto the framework.

Essentially, the journey begins in the hero's home, then takes him off on an adventure in which he does battle until finally returning home, weary yet triumphant, as a stronger character. As you consider how you'd like your life to pan out, here are the most important stages that unfold in every hero's story:

» *The call to adventure* – our hero begins in the ordinary world where he often denies or refuses to hear the call to adventure. He stays in his comfort zone until he can stay there no longer.

» *Meeting a mentor* – our hero meets someone to help him, a teacher or guide who will show him the way forward.

» *Crossing the threshold* – our hero takes the first brave step. He has accepted the challenge.

» *The road of trials* – our hero undergoes a series of ordeals that test him to the limit and meets a mixture of allies and enemies on the way until he achieves his goal or reward.

» *Returning to the ordinary world with the elixir* – finally our hero heads home, personally transformed by the experience.

The story of your experience at school, wrenched from home and out into the world is an example of a hero's journey. So too is any stage of your life where you undertake a new journey – accept a new job, leave home to set up with a new partner, take up a new hobby. It involves heeding that call to the next adventure, and bravely stepping over the familiar threshold into the unknown.

The first and most difficult step is to make a commitment to yourself to own all of your life, being fully responsible for yourself and the results you get. Only then can you reclaim your personal life and enrich your professional one.

As lawyer Steve realised, 'I have to make a commitment to myself, to own my life, because nobody else is going to take responsibility for it. Lawyer is only one of the hats I wear, and I was investing too much of my life into that one role. When I saw how some of the partners in the firm were just waiting for retirement to live, then I woke up and realised that my life is about what happens today, not in the future.'

Exercise

Your hero's journey today

You are the hero in your own life; now's the chance to develop your personal script. The starting point on any journey is to begin to assess your home surroundings and what is calling to you.

Imagine for a moment that the short story of how you live one aspect of your life and your work was captured in this book. What would it say about you? Here are some prompts:

» Think about the different roles that you take on in your life, not just work ones.

» Consider some of the best of times and the worst of times for you.

» Where is there any conflict or tension for you at work?

» How content are you with your home life? What might be even better?

» What is calling you to an adventure right now?

» What is the threshold you need to step over? Is this barrier within you or about the people around you?

» Who are some of the allies, enemies or mentors you have met or would like to meet on your journey?

Now spend just ten minutes writing about your life and work as it is today in just a few paragraphs including a current challenge or possibility for you, which has some energy and importance. Take a blank piece of paper to create your story, or jot the highlights here in the book. (If words don't work for you, collect some coloured pens and create your story in a drawing.) The story is for your eyes only, so it's OK to allow the words to tumble out without being perfect.

My story today...

Looking at your story, consider whether yours is an attractive and enticing life; one that others would like to lead. What else do you notice as you read your own story? Consider how you'd like it to evolve as you travel through the book so that later you can write it as your legacy story in Chapter 5 – the tale of what you have actually done.

As heroes in our own lives, there will naturally be tension between our different roles because we have a finite amount of time in the day and our energy gets spread wide. How many women struggle to be a wonderful homemaker and business person, a caring daughter as well as a traveller of the world? How many men feel they need to be the good provider yet dream of a life adventure that takes them far from home or a secure job?

Playing many different roles **simultaneously** on the world's stage causes overload in a solo act. You are left wondering who you are to the point of freezing in your tracks, putting your life on hold and doing nothing – until you have the money, your children are grown up, your elderly parents no longer need you. The problem with this approach is that we have one life and no second chances. Months of stretching in different directions turn to years, turn to decades.

The only sane way forward is to stop battling and accept reality, by acknowledging the tensions each role brings. Stop 'trying' to perfect each one simultaneously; there can be no perfect balance between all these roles at the same time; the peace comes from a deeper place within yourself.

There's a paradox at work whereby the goal-setting, goal-getting measures of achievement also involve us surrendering to what is happening around us rather than being able to control it all. If we're aiming to raise the 'success' bar all the time, going for bigger and bigger challenges that are potentially exhausting, it's worth starting from a simple place of contentment, going with the moment and moving gracefully over one foot or three foot hurdles to help prepare you for the challenge.

ACCESSING ENERGY

Getting in touch with your energy involves exercising new parts of yourself. When you are operating from your core position of strength without interference, all your energy is aligned and moving freely; all your senses are focused outwards from a strong central point. When part of you tries to split your attention by heading in a new or contrasting direction, then it creates an inner tension and your whole system needs to adapt.

Exercise

Feel the energy

Let's pause a moment while I invite you to stretch out one of your hands. Look at your hand with the palm uppermost and stretch all five digits of that hand as far out as is comfortable, really watching, feeling, moving your fingers and thumb. Get a sense of the space between each finger and the energy shifting out to the very tips of the fingers. When you are doing this, the energy through your hand is flowing freely from the core of your palm. It's strong and aligned. Experience that as you move your fingers back and forward.

Now try bending each finger in turn towards the centre of your palm, and see what happens to the stretch. Notice how comfortable it is to isolate one finger and stretch out the others. Maybe when your thumb moves in towards the palm, the stretch is still reasonable. As you bend your ring finger or middle finger, for example, I suspect it's not quite so easy to keep the other four digits fully stretched out – you will be bringing in some tension; the energy's no longer flowing so freely.

Consider your hand as a symbol for the whole of you and your life. If you want to have hands that are flexible, then clearly you need to exercise each part, regularly stretching to the edge and then relaxing without bending too far backwards. Each and every part of your hand needs to work as a complete system, each respecting the integrity of the whole.

We lose the ability to access and top up our energy when we lose a sense of space in our lives. Energy is multi-dimensional and created in different ways for each of us; those lines need to be free-flowing for us to live the life we really want to live.

Every aspect of our life takes a different quality of energy. It is possible to stay sane and reclaim your life by paying attention to different dimensions of your energy and keeping these areas topped up healthily.

Check in with your own energy and rate how you are today in the following exercise.

Exercise

Personal Energy Audit

Give yourself a score from one to ten on each factor that indicates your current satisfaction in this area. One is low and ten is high. For each section you will get a maximum score of 60.

Physical Energy

» As you go through your day, how would you rate your level of 'bounce' from lazy at the low end of the scale to full of beans at the top?

» Are you eating regular nutritious food every day and drinking plenty of water?

» Do you get as much sleep as you need? How would you rate the quality?

» Have you a way of getting regular exercise each week?

» Does your schedule build in time for you to relax with nothing you have to do?

» Can you get through the day without more than one cup of tea or coffee?

Sub-total: __/60

Mental Energy

» Does your work fully utilise your skills and talents?

....

» Are you enthusiastic about what you do and working in line with your
  personal priorities?

....

» Are you relatively free of anxiety as you go about your work rather than
  stressed or overwhelmed much of the time?

....

» Do you feel you are continually learning and growing?

....

» When faced with a shock, can you recover fast and turn it into an opportunity?

....

» Do you have engrossing hobbies that give you 'me time' and a complete
  break from work?

....

Sub-total: __/60

(continued)

Emotional Energy

» Do you feel that relationships with those around you are honest and respectful of you as an individual?

» Do you manage to stay centred and calm in the midst of conflict situations?

» Do you feel you can rise above feelings of guilt, fear and anger?

» Do you find it easy to say 'no' when someone asks you to do something that doesn't match what you want to do?

» Do you feel joyful and content most of the time?

» Do you recognise the triggers that can affect your change in mood?

Sub-total: __/60

Purposeful Energy

» Do you feel that you are spending your time on activities that are meaningful and useful?

....

» Do you have a sense of purposefulness as you go about your daily life?

....

» Do you connect with nature, the great outdoors on a regular basis?

....

» Are you clear on your values, what is really important to you?

....

» Do you have a sense of where you fit or contribute within a larger community of people?

....

» Are you comfortable that you can be yourself without undue concern for what other people think of you?

....

Sub-total: __/60

How to use the audit

Each of the sections here relates to one of four key energy dimensions that we'll be exploring in the following chapters.

1. Physical

2. Mental

3. Emotional

4. Purposeful

Make a note of your scores for each section and make a diary note to come back to them in a few weeks' time to see how your energy is recovering as you put the ideas and exercises from the book into practice. Physical energy lays the foundation for your health and is the most ignored aspect of professionals' lives; this is the first area to look at. However, if your scores are low on one of the other dimensions, you might like to jump ahead to the appropriate chapter for inspiration before coming back to the physical aspects.

Four dimensions of energy

When we follow our energy intuitively and logically, we naturally shift to work that sings to our soul as well as loving the life that we create for ourselves. This doesn't mean to say it will be perfect all of the time, but at least we know where it has gone off track and what needs to happen for us to get focused once more on where we want to be.

The following chapters of the book address the four dimensions of energy.

1 *Physical energy:* It goes without saying that when we're well, we can conquer the world; we're buzzing, energetic, enthusiastic and attractive to others. Physical health is the foundation for life, and easy to take for granted until the body fails in some way. Without your health you're in trouble – you don't feel alive. Physical wellbeing starts by fuelling the body with good quality food and water that converts to energy. It involves taking sufficient exercise: relevant activities to strengthen muscles and good quality relaxation and sleep.

2 *Mental energy:* Mental energy relates to using your intellectual powers with the optimum level of variety and challenge. It's about recognising when you are in a state

of 'flow' that leaves you fully engrossed and content with the job in hand. To function at your mental best involves harnessing all parts of the brain – at both the conscious and unconscious level. When you give yourself 'downtime' with hobbies and interests that boost your creativity, you feed your ability to take on tough logical challenges too.

3 *Emotional energy:* Do your emotions govern you, or do you govern them? When we are emotionally strong, we have a highly tuned awareness of ourselves and what triggers our emotions. Equally, we are sensitive to the needs of others, and able to develop strong, empathic relationships. We are able to even out the peaks and troughs that form regular daily life.

4 *Purposeful energy:* Life without meaning and purpose becomes hard to sustain. Some people have a clear sense of direction and purpose; others know what feels right to them. Purposeful energy enables you to make meaning and connections in your life so that it feels 'spirited' and worthwhile. You know that you make a difference, just by being who you are.

YOU DESERVE PLAYTIME

When people talk about the happy times in their childhood, invariably we hear carefree stories of play and freedom, of playing outdoors in the street, the park, the fields and the beach. There's a sense of excitement at being part of an engrossing world.

As we move into the world of work, initially full of enthusiasm, there comes a crunch time when we notice that the fun has stopped. In its place, the drudgery of delivering projects, budgets or appraisals kicks in along with anxieties and the responsibility of working with people who behave badly or treat their colleagues as a robotic resource.

In the words of one colleague, Ian: 'It's the de-sensitisation that's hard to swallow.' After experiencing several takeover situations, he says: 'The idea that customers are at the heart of what we do becomes a big lie as the systems no longer allow it. We have to tick the boxes for the systems first, and can't do the best thing or make the right decisions.'

At one time his life and work was completely entwined. 'I have worked in aggressive sales organisations that want the single-minded, focused, "get the deal" mindset, and that becomes a brutal existence to live with year in and year out.'

The loss of fun in the rough and tumble detracts from the reason why we chose to do the work we love or to be in that business in the first place. Work becomes a heavy burden, tiring to hold. The mentality kicks in that 'if it's not SERIOUS, then it's not real work.'

Thought provoker

One question to ask yourself to help open up a new quality to work is : 'Am I getting enough playtime?' When you look in your diary and identify the breaks, ask yourself: 'Where is the real fun here?' How much time out which is not task-focused do you get? Are you happy with what you see in your schedule? Have the hours devoted to work crept up on you or become so intense that there is no downtime?

Playtime for adults, as well as kids, is about having the space to fully enjoy the moment, to feel free right at your core. You know there are things you could always be doing elsewhere – jobs, chores or more work. Yet right now you're simply having fun being in the moment.

Happy workers make the day-to-day tasks fun in some way, so that the work flows easily and the pressure is lightened. You may choose to work long hours – that's less of a problem when there's humour and fun involved – but also recognise the need to take time out where no work is allowed in. We all need time with no email access or phone contact with clients; time to just hang out, listen to music, walk and read, do whatever we need for pure pleasure with no work agenda in mind.

Many dedicated professionals find it easier to allow others to play than to give themselves the permission to do so. 'I get paid a lot of money so it's OK for me to work long hours,' is a common message. These are often the same people who believe they deserve less time off than those who earn less than they do. If you're struggling to take time out for yourself, it's worth pausing to understand what it would take for you to give yourself permission to find that sense of space so essential to re-charge.

Do it today

Each day that Bev goes to work, she sees the reality of the length of a person's life; the physical evidence is there in front of her eyes, knowing that we all end up the same way in death. Bev's work is as a director in her family's funeral business. Her motto for living life is: 'Don't put things off.'

One of the reasons that she can handle clients' grief with sensitivity and respect is that she has strong boundaries around her work, and recognises that she cannot take ownership of other people's pain. She works four long days each week, takes one day off and books regular holidays; she gives herself permission to play. Unlike many business owners, she doesn't get so tied up in work that play gets lost. She loves parties, travel, sport, entertaining and her family life to the point that people are surprised when she tells them what her job is, dismissing the perception that you would have be a wizened elderly gentleman to be a funeral director. She recognises that: 'I couldn't do this job if I took it home with me.'

When at work, she gives her complete focus and professional attention to the job in hand. 'I give myself a few goals at a time, not massive ones, then concentrate on doing the important things today.'

As a working mother she says she inevitably has 101 things to do at work and another 101 at home. 'I really like to be busy and I'm not tolerant of anyone around me whingeing.' She applies the same 'can do' enthusiasm to hobbies like playing tennis or scuba diving. 'Whatever I do, I like to see progress, and I never give up, although contrary to most people, I like to start with the things I like doing most and that keeps me in a good mood.'

As adults we all need playtime to re-charge our batteries in comfort and peace without a care in the world. Our playtime is about a distinct space where our responsibilities can be set aside, where we can run free with a sense of the timeless joy in the moment.

Check out where in your life you can do this and with whom. Where do you truly laugh and giggle? Can you get this by simply walking in the park or by the river in your lunch break, packing a picnic lunch instead of eating a hasty sandwich at your desk, eating outside and feeling the sun or wind on your face? It costs us nothing but the willingness to step for a period of time from the seriousness of our work to play.

Top tip

Block your playtime in your diary and keep it sacred: just like it was at school. Start with 15 minutes twice a day, every day, at a time that fits your schedule.

As we create more space, so we begin to break the pattern of long working hours that many professionals have got into. By shrinking the time spent on the less enjoyable parts of our work, we begin to change our relationship with it, enriching the experience and getting our lives back. It means that we re-focus on doing the right things, and evolve our work to make it a neater fit.

As you give yourself time to play more, to vent your creativity, and make this your focus, then the quality of your relationship with work changes – it becomes healthier and sustainable.

Dream jobs

The idea of more playtime appealed to John. His dream job would be to play sax in a band, yet he is committed to his formal job in hospital management which pays the mortgage. He builds two 15-minute slots dedicated to his music-making into each day. On some days that will be playing time, on others he'll walk outside the office and listen to the MP3 sound files he's recorded on his music player.

John's profile with his team changed as he revealed his musical talent. Recently, he surprised his team by playing the sax at an off-site team building session and led by example, showing that he believed it's important to have other interests in your life than work.

In her role as a PA, Debbie dreams of the day when she'll be a published novelist. For now she's translating the stresses of train commuting to her advantage by building daily fantasies about fellow travellers into characters for her fiction. Her paid job has its uses, too, as she's developing her IT skills learning about blogging, twittering and websites, building a community of potential readers for her novels. She may never become a great novelist and that's not the point. Just for the moment she is allowing herself to have more fun.

Change often happens in small steps. Opportunities for a new dimension to your work begin by allowing more time to play.

LISTEN TO YOUR INTUITION

The business world thrives on detailed, logical thinking, precision and performance. Business dictates tangible results. So, we get caught up with a particular way of thinking about life – the 'group think' mentality of 'This is how it has to be' – that there is a real danger of burn-out from stress from intense and detailed work, as we'll see shortly in lawyer Steve's story and thousands like him.

The one person who can make the change is you and in order to open up choices for yourself, you need to be able to access more of yourself, the intuitive, creative parts that get lost because they are undervalued. Through the pages of this book I'll be encouraging you to find ways to access your true and authentic self, the part that hides in the shadows lost in the fray of work and a busy life.

Logic derives from conscious thinking while intuitive thinking accesses a much richer source of knowledge – your unconscious, sub-conscious or 'other than conscious' processing power.

Carl Jung described intuition as 'perception via the unconscious', suggesting that intuition bypasses our relatively slow conscious thinking processes and draws on everything that we have in our unconscious or subconscious mind in an instant. Just think that our knowledge, memories and experiences are there ready and waiting without us having to consciously remember them.

Jung also said that 'intuition is the ability to perceive possibilities, implications and principles without the burden of detail'. So our intuition works with the big picture – our hopes and dreams – leaving the practical details for our conscious minds to figure out. For those who need detail plus hard facts and figures to back up an argument, it's hard to follow a 'hunch'.

The business world trains us on the logical path, yet entrepreneurial businesses value the intuitive dimension of listening to the gut reaction. Similarly, in designing the course of our own lives, when we find ways to step beyond the dominance of logic and notice the additional messages from the more creative part of ourselves, we are likely to be more 'successful' in living lives that fit us better.

Opening up possibilities

Creative sessions that involve art, drama, storytelling, humour, yoga, meditation, music and dance open us up to new possibilities. For example, in her workshops on 'The Art of Intuition' Angela O'Connell encourages people to play with paint on wet art paper, choosing the colours that appeal and dropping some amounts of colour onto the page and allowing whatever needs to emerge, to come. The act of painting quietens the logical mind and participants are able to interpret their art to get new information on their life direction. Once the paint has settled, she invites participants to talk about the personal meaning they take from their paintings.

By taking part in one of Angela's workshops, I realised I wanted to take people out of their normal working environments to retreats and events that gave them time to think clearly. Another participant decided he would base his family and business from his holiday home in Turkey where he now has several wonderful holiday properties.

By not being open to his intuition, lawyer Steve felt he paid the price of losing three years of his life: 'I was so caught up in the system and busy doing work to keep others happy that I didn't pay any attention to the gut message. In fact I didn't want to hear it. After all, how could I tell my family or boss that I wasn't coping?'

Intuition is a gift that allows us to pay attention to what's working or not and find our natural wisdom. Fear of making changes or upsetting others can get in the way. Being over-busy limits the quality of our experience and defeats the objectives we're trying to achieve.

The power of the unconscious mind is so much greater than the conscious mind.

TECHNOLOGY – FROM FRIEND TO FOE

Ostensibly technology improves the quality of our work and lives. We are beeped and tweeted, pinged, nudged and mailed, as well as phoned on our PCs, mobiles and landlines. Twenty years ago, the workplace was full of physical mail trays overloaded with paper: today, it's a novelty to receive a business letter. In my roles in the IT industry, I spent years telling customers how technology could solve their problems and extolled the virtues of connecting with the world. 'Ha, ha,' we joked that people would even be accessible in the bathroom; today such constant accessibility is true and beyond a joke.

It's a fine line that tips our work from exciting and purposeful activity into addiction. Technology does not always do us a favour.

Switched off

Steve was on a top talent career ladder in a law firm where the pressure was on to take on heavy long-term case loads. After three years on one case, he reached the point where he felt he had to check and answer email and text messages from his divisional partner from the time he woke up until the time he went to bed. A single man, living alone, he had no-one to share cooking with and was living on a diet of orange juice, chocolate, grapes and take-away burgers.

He felt nauseous with worry when he couldn't get through his work in regular hours and was overcome with sheer panic. Often the time between switching off the PC until turning it back on shrank to four hours, and he was accessible online for the other 20 hours. Bombarded by messages that requested action from his boss, he had become the proverbial 'worker ant'.

Like so many in that situation, he was the last person to realise how the situation had got out of hand until, taking a rare weekend off to visit his brother, he collapsed with stomach pains and exhaustion. 'I forgot how to switch off, and only learnt the hard way how important this is.'

The price we pay for connections

Technology makes the world a smaller place and we've bought into it at a price. The price we pay is to be continually distracted and interrupted (if we allow it). There's even a new field of knowledge known as 'interruption science.' For all our smart devices and connections, our attention is fragmented and our focus on one thing at a time is completely lost.

According to Gloria Mark, a leader in this field, the average knowledge-worker – that is, someone whose work is based on intellectual ability – switches task every three minutes and, once distracted, that worker takes nearly 30 minutes to get back to the original task. So the impact on the professionals who are making decisions that affect all of us – from our pension funds to the drugs we take – is massive. No wonder people feel frustrated, pressured and stressed out.

To think creatively and intelligently, we need non-interrupted time, and that time is under threat in our digital age. It's up to us to use technology intelligently as our support system without allowing it to drive us. Taking time out without phones and computers is a massive challenge for those of us used to being connected. When the online connections go down or our mobile phones get lost, how bereft can we feel?

FIND PEACE AND FREEDOM

Achieving a strong and constant sense of control over our lives is impossible when the world around us is changing all the time. The thousands of hours I've spent listening to people have taught me that, ultimately, what people want is a sense of peace and the personal freedom to make the right choices concerning how they live and what they do – for themselves, their families, and their colleagues. These are fundamental values for the hardest working person.

The call of the sea

As a manager in a Financial Services business, Jan told me through our coaching work that he'd often felt a sense of frustration with the systems at work, where he dreams of chucking in his job and opening a surf shack in Cornwall. Part of him yearns for the freedom and simplicity that the beach and sea bring.

Yet as we explored that real possibility – what would happen if he did this – he decided that a major relocation wouldn't bring him the satisfaction he gets from his work: he'd get bored with salt and sand.

Like so many over-stretched, high achievers, Jan survived from one holiday to the next. It's an all too familiar tale, to be on a treadmill with relentless deadlines – always another client whose urgent project demands working into the evening and weekends. Holidays were his only times to switch off and have fun. Life can go on hold for nearly fifty weeks of the year in the 'busyness' of making a living.

As he dreamt of escaping the business world and the sea beckoned, I invited him to become curious about how he could bring more of this dream world into his everyday work and life so that he could reclaim his life rather than walking away from all the knowledge and people skills he had invested in. How could he enrich his work, making it fun and rewarding, and a great place to be for all?

Over the period of a year, Jan cultivated a greater sense of freedom in his day-to-day life. Now he's adopted rituals each week that include checking that his diary has space for him to enjoy simpler pleasures. He pays attention to his energy levels and knows what triggers a dip, reminding himself of the choices he has made and approaching each day with gratitude for the adventure.

He's changed his physical working and home environment to create lighter spaces with neutral walls, natural woods and stunning images of favourite surf beaches. His diet has lightened up too and he's building team walks by the river for thinking time and team meetings. In January, he books regular long weekends for the family throughout the year at surfing locations in the UK and abroad.

SANITY AS YOU GO

You can create sanity instead of slavery in your work and have a smoother time as you go. The choice is not between working and not working, yet it does mean some tough thinking about what is truly important to you and letting go of things you'd still like to do in order to evolve the way you work. Work sanity is about continually fine tuning and making choices that are right for you and your situation today.

There is no single easy or magic plan to increase the levels of happiness you feel in your life and work. Your life situation is unique to you and you may well feel stretched or confused by the choices you have to make when you want to have and do it all. What is most important is to listen to yourself from the inside as well as to the external signals from friends and family, colleagues, clients and bosses. Allow sanity to prevail.

Achieving a balance between your professional and private life is a misnomer; life is a mix, a blend, a long-term relationship that accommodates aspects of you and your changing needs and those of others. Only you can manage this relationship for yourself in your own delightful way.

CHAPTER 2

PHYSICAL ENERGY

Quit the Toxic Substances

Tune Into Your Body

Wake Up to Health

Build in Recovery Time

Operate Boundary Control

Disconnect the Drainers

Create New Rituals

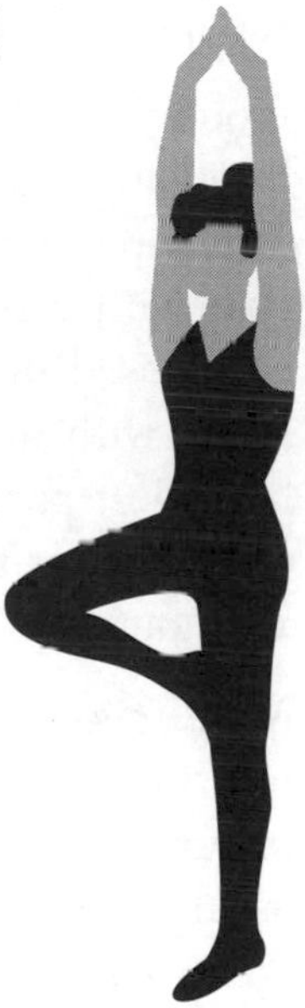

D o you have days when you can't wait to jump out of bed in the morning, when you feel alive and excited about what lies ahead; and others when you can't quite summon up the energy to swing your toes onto the floor – when you're yearning for a 'duvet day?'

It's natural to experience variations in energy levels. On some days you will be raring to go and give life your best perform-ance, and on others you need to rest and recover. However, feeling persistently tired and worn down or constantly hyped up are signals that your energy levels are off-balance and you need to pay attention to your physical health.

Taking good care of your physical self by paying close atten-tion to good nutrition and regular exercise will not only increase your energy levels but will also enable you to make the most of life's opportunities.

Good health builds personal resilience. Resilient people listen attentively to their bodies and are more likely to steer a healthy course. They know they need to balance exer-tion with rest; that coffee, alcohol and junk food should be enjoyed in moderation. They manage their blood sugar levels with appropriate nutrition and exercise. Often the healthiest people have learnt the hard way, through burn-out or a health crisis, that physical energy really matters. Without physical energy you can't live life to the full.

Many people are caught up in a vicious cycle. They feel too tired to do anything about their health – they're stuck in survival mode rather than thriving. Physical tiredness is usually entwined with emotional fatigue which compounds the problem.

This chapter looks at why physical energy is important and offers practical ways to improve the quality of your everyday life. The effort involved doesn't have to be massive. It is more a case of introducing simple steps to fine tune your daily habits, such as: planning each day's healthy meals in advance; building a 15-minute walk into your commute or school run; turning off the computer and playing a game of cards instead; drinking a glass of fruit juice instead of having another cup of tea; limiting your time with people who drain you.

The art of managing physical energy is to even out the peaks and troughs of exertion. The aim is to achieve a baseline state that is calm and relaxed in which the exertion of performing is balanced by the discipline of recovery.

QUIT THE TOXIC SUBSTANCES

Just walk around any supermarket to see the amount of shelf space allocated for ready meals, beer and wines. Petrol stations are loaded with giant-sized packs of sweets, crisps and fizzy drinks. Visit a typical coffee shop chain and you will find the staff geared up to promote the sale of large shots of caffeine with an accompanying treat loaded with sugar and fat to go with it.

Increasing levels of obesity and incidence of Type 2 diabetes are causes for concern for government ministers and the health service professionals who have to budget for the cost of unhealthy lifestyles. Much of the data shows an increase in our sugar consumption (including alcohol) and reduced levels of exercise.

Experts suggest that diabetes is the biggest challenge to our health today. Cardiovascular disease is the most common complication, which accounts for at least half of the 70 deaths attributable to diabetes every day.

As a primary school teacher looking after 30 youngsters, Linda needs to be on the ball at all times. She has lost several stone in weight and looks and feels more energetic than she has for ten years. The arrival of a new child in her class fired the trigger she needed to make changes to her own diet and exercise regime. She explained: 'When I witnessed the effect that one digestive biscuit had on a diabetic child in my class, I decided it was time to get rid of sugar in my diet. He went from a real low dip to a high within minutes.'

Doing a bit of research showed Linda that her treats – the occasional cigarette, several cups of strong coffee and wine with dinner each night – were leading to long-term risks. She eats no sugar, avoids stimulants like cola, coffee and wine, and has instigated walks at lunchtime with her colleagues instead of munching flapjacks together in the staff room.

Maintaining stable blood sugar levels is the basis of healthy eating programmes such as the low GL diet from Patrick Holford, founder of the Institute of Nutrition. GL refers to Glycaemic Load. It is a way of measuring the quantity and quality of carbohydrate in a given food – how fast carbohydrates are converted into sugar. Foods with a high GL rating burn sugar fast and encourage the body to store fat; foods with a low GL rating burn it slowly and encourage the body to burn fat. Over the last 20 years, Holford has inspired thousands of people with his intelligent and well researched approach to nutrition.

When blood sugar levels are unstable, the result is a feeling of anxiety as well as exhaustion and weight gain. Reaching

PEAKS ▶ Affects arteries & insulin production

STABLE LEVELS
= Steady energy supply

DIPS ▶ Affects tiredness & concentration

Uneven levels of blood sugar increase the stress on the body and weight gain. **Peaks** damage arteries and release excess insulin. **Dips** affect tiredness and concentration.

Stable levels create a steady supply of energy.

for sweets to cheer us up when we're worried has the opposite effect to the one intended. When the brain senses that blood sugar is low, it sends a hormonal message to pour adrenalin into the system; this raises blood sugar once more, but also heightens our fears. Adrenalin sends the Sympathetic Nervous System into a state of high alert – triggering the classic fight/flight reaction, which causes the heart to palpitate, the stomach to churn and blood vessels to dilate.

The good news is that we can choose to make some simple adjustments in diet and lifestyle that switch off the impulse to run on adrenalin all the time, as Angie found out.

Cutting back from pasta and pesto

Fit, fashionable and fast-moving, 35-year-old Angie describes working as a London-based recruitment consultant in her 20s. She worked late into the evening calling candidates, survived on 4–5 hours sleep, snacked on white pasta and pesto and went for early morning runs and early evening gym classes. Four nights a week she'd socialise, trying out the new clubs and bars, partying interspersed with whirl-wind shopping weekends and ski trips. Thumping her fist three times into her palm, she sums up the speed as 'Boom-Boom-Boom. I was an incredible adrenalin junkie.'

After a split from her boyfriend she realised that the pace was leading to certain burn-out. Feeling constantly exhausted, she took the decision to chuck in her job and return to her native Scotland. 'I had a vision that all would be wonderful if I went back home to a quiet place and a quiet job.'

Within two weeks Angie remembered the reasons she had headed south. In her haste to bolt to safety she'd forgotten what she valued. 'I missed my friends, my flat, the gym, the good weather and the sheer buzz. I could walk to work in my new job in Scotland yet I felt compelled to push people along the street. They were like snails.'

Angie was left feeling lethargic and bored. 'I need to be stretched. I thrive on enthusiasm and a level of pace. The shift from the crazy fast to the painfully slow was too extreme for me.'

Within a few months Angie headed back South, this time making small yet significant adjustments in her choice of home and job, holding on to what was important to her. She now lives in a cottage within easy access of London, with fields virtually on her doorstep and a buzzing local community. She's shifted into corporate HR work that rarely intrudes into her evenings and weekends, sleeps longer, eats proper meals and has expanded her love of exercise to cycling and marathon running. She's cut back on the addictive socialising and 'out of hours' work.

Although that move to Scotland was disastrous at the time, it provided a good learning curve. 'I got much clearer on what is working and what isn't, so that I fine-tune things rather than overlooking the good aspects in my impatience. It's important to slow down enough that you can ask yourself more questions and do more planning instead of jumping from one extreme to another when you're under stress.'

Top tip

Habits develop over the months and years. Buy yourself a notebook and simply write down everything you eat and drink and all the exercise you do – every day. The discipline of measuring draws your attention to what is happening. This is the first step in making adjustments.

TUNE IN TO YOUR BODY

When we're busy working hard, it's easy to override physical warnings and disregard the messages from our bodies. Only when we stop working do we notice how we really feel. This is why so many people get migraines on Saturday mornings or spend their holidays ill in bed.

Sometimes the oversight is accidental and the decline is gradual, rather like a garden that becomes slowly overrun with ivy as it shoots through the borders and climbs the walls. At other times, pressure of work leads to a deliberate decision to turn a blind eye to ill-health: how inconvenient it is to be sick, especially when you have a business to run. A managing director of a firm of accountants once said to me: 'I haven't time for the operation I'm supposed to have.' Once an illness takes root, it will need serious attention to restore the body to health again.

Illness is characterised by pain and anything in our lives that persistently creates pain will ultimately damage our health; staying healthy means becoming clever at tuning into the source of our energy within our physical body. It involves finding practices like meditation and yoga that offer ways to recognise what it's like to be truly calm, centred and healthy, so that we immediately notice the effect on our bodies when life is more challenging and we take speedy action to restore the body to good health.

Good physical health can't be separated from emotional and mental wellbeing; it begins with regular exercise and good diet. Our levels of confidence and personal motivation have an impact on physical wellbeing.

When people are engaged in work that doesn't fit with their strengths, or lack sufficient training or support to do their jobs, they can become physically ill. A client came to me for advice about the anxiety attacks he suffered when asked to put anything in writing. Whenever asked for documentation, he felt weak and headed for chocolate. He knew that writing wasn't his core skill, yet was reluctant to admit this to his colleagues. He felt he had to be a fluent writer in order to hold down his role as leader of a customer service team. Once this client accepted that he could get practical help to improve his skills, then his anxiety went away and he reduced his chocolate consumption.

In order to thrive in any organisation it is necessary to understand the company culture, and to recognise 'what it's like around here'. If you know what's expected of you, you can decide whether the prevailing culture is a good fit for your identity and whether it enables you to work at your best. If you can't make it work smoothly, then you are in the wrong place. To prevent getting physically ill, you will need either to change your approach or shift to another organisation.

Knowing the rules of the corporate world

As a senior manager with a long-term career in a technology company, Neil describes how he learnt the rules of the organisation over time. 'Essentially, I'm a commodity resource, and I keep that knowledge in the back of my mind: I know I'm dispensable.' He describes the need to make a profit to be as natural as breathing: 'If I don't make a profit, then I don't exist here – there's no job for me.'

Back in his 20s and 30s Neil felt he had to immerse himself in work to the exclusion of all else. He worked hard, socialised with his team and was rarely at home. 'I saw myself as "Mr Provider" for the family, which iron-ically meant I was so driven to succeed that I let my career manage me.'

When his wife left with the children and asked for a divorce, the shock hit Neil both physically and emotionally. He tried to deal with solici-tors, and move home while still travelling through Europe for work. He was eating too much, drinking too much and became, in his own words, a '17-stone curry muncher' who worked too hard and slept too little. After one international flight, he collapsed, requiring hospital care at risk of heart failure. It was the wake-up call he needed.

Fortunately, he worked for an organisation that was supportive. His boss immediately gave him time off as well as external support in the form of therapy and medical care. Once he admitted what he was going through, he found numerous colleagues rallied round as they too had been through tough times. 'I learnt it's OK to cry and admit that "It's not fine. I can't do this any more." And also that recovery isn't instant. I thought I'd be better in a week or two but it took a couple of months.'

Looking at him now – fit and well and many stones lighter, it's hard to imagine him at his most unhealthy. He took up running and working out in the gym and lost a few stone. Today, Neil trains and competes in cycling events, giving him the physical energy to take on challenging work.

It took the difficult times for Neil to establish new healthier rituals that protect him from burn-out. The benefit is that they also set an example to his team to make healthy working a priority. Here are his personal principles that ensure he loves his work and still lives life.

1. *Plan to exercise – 'At the start of each week, book the 30-minute to one hour spaces when you will be exercising.'*

2. *Never book your diary back to back. 'My worst nightmare is a conference that means being with people from breakfast to dinner.'*

3. *Work when you're at work. Be home when you're home. 'Set clear boundaries, even though there will be long hours at times.'*

4. *Be comfortable with leaving the office while others are still working. 'I have no problems saying that I'm going now.'*

5. *Live for today – 'I used to virtually plan for pipe and slippers by the time I was 50. Now I like to be spontaneous and enjoy every minute.'*

WAKE UP TO HEALTH

Enlightened organisations place employee health high on their agenda; they introduce training programmes that show people how to increase their wellbeing with practical ideas to encourage good habits. They have paid attention to data on health and understand that unhealthy employees represent a commercial risk to the business. Low levels of exercise and poor nutrition lead people to simply lose focus and concentration, however personally motivated they are to succeed.

Between 2006 and 2008, the pharmaceutical giant, GSK, put 3000 employees in 30 countries through its 'Energy for Performance' programme. They had found that physical energy was by far the most neglected aspect of executives' lives. By offering support for putting in place new healthy habits, over 80 per cent of people reported an improvement in mental or physical performance; with a lift in energy of over 50 per cent that was sustained over a 12-month period.

Not many people are fortunate enough to have this kind of support from an employer. Health programmes are seen more generally as an optional extra, rather than essential. When business gets tough and pressure builds, the fallout usually impacts on individual employees. Underperformers are all too easily replaced by the next person queuing for their job. The message is, if we don't take personal responsibility for our own health, whether we are carers or chief executives, no-one else will.

When I hear of increasing levels of stress, heart failure, and fatigue-related illnesses causing people to crash out of work, it's a personal wake-up call too. Any one of us whose role involves supporting customers, clients or loved ones needs to hold on to the thought: 'When I look after me first, then I can look after you.'

Your physical energy action plan

Activity is a natural way of being for some people – they simply can't sit still. For others who gravitate towards relaxing in a comfy chair with the remote control, a change of habit is called for! When we're active, the benefits are enormous:

1. **Metabolic rate** – speeds up through activity, so you burn fat faster.
2. **Appetite** – is reduced. Those who exercise more or use up more physical energy through their work eat proportionately less than their sedentary counterparts.
3. **Health** – is increased by stabilising blood sugar levels and controlling weight.

To get fitter, it's not necessary to join the gym, take a class or swallow up hours of your time. Fitness experts advise us to exercise for just 15 minutes every day or for 35 minutes three times a week. Choose a mix of aerobic exercise to raise the heart rate and muscle building to burn fat. It is important to warm up and cool down with Yoga or Pilates-type moves too.

Top tips to get active

Stop	Start
✕ Meeting for lunch	✓ Meeting for a walk and talk
✕ Taking the lift or escalator	✓ Taking the stairs
✕ Sending emails round the office	✓ Speaking in person
✕ Taking the bus or tube/metro	✓ Walking part of the way
✕ Watching TV	✓ Finding a physical hobby like gardening, sport or dancing

---

Developing body awareness

The art of listening is possibly the most valuable skill we develop in life. Yet how good are we at really listening at a deep level to the wisdom of our bodies? Buddhist Alan Ashley advocates the value of simple meditation exercises for checking what is going on in our bodies and how we are feeling.

Meditation allows us to get calm and focused. It's like coming back to a baseline starting point on a tennis court instead of playing each shot from where we hit the last one.

Exercise

A daily meditation practice

You can do this exercise wherever you are and whatever is going on – at work as well as at home. When you have time, go systematically through the body, at other times just tune into key aspects of your experience.

Getting into position

There are two important principles in meditation that are reflected in posture: the aspects of calm, receptivity, and relaxation need to be complemented by alertness and clarity of intention. This means that a meditation posture needs to allow you to relax without drifting off to sleep and to be alert without becoming tense or uncomfortable.

If you choose to sit on cushions, ensure that you have a very stable foundation: if you cannot get your knees down to the ground when sitting cross-legged then it is probably best to sit astride the cushions. If you use a chair, try to ensure that your back is as upright as possible, your feet are about hip width apart and your knees are about level with your hips.

Support your hands and arms, otherwise they might constrict your chest and make it difficult to breathe.

The full practice

Gradually pay attention to each part of your body in turn, taking time to really notice each part rather than just thinking about it. It may help to talk your way through the practice internally, saying to yourself 'noticing my feet... the toes... the soles... the arches...' and so on. Take time to notice any sensations, making sure to leave gaps between the phrases.

Gradually work your way up your legs, up your back, around your head and face and down your arms. Then bring your attention to your belly, breathing down into it to allow it to soften, then to your solar plexus (just below the sternum) and to your heart area. The sensations in this part of the body will usually help you to connect with your feelings. Remember, there is no particular experience you ought to be having; however you feel or don't feel is absolutely fine.

Now notice the thinking bit of your mind, doing your best to observe thoughts without getting caught up in them. This is sometimes known as 'being on the balcony', so you watch your thoughts as though they are people moving in a dance, without being part of the 'dance' yourself.

The brief practice

In the workplace, it can be fruitful to simply notice your connection with the ground, through your feet and weight on your chair. Then notice the uplift and support of your spine, and conclude by breathing down into the belly and allowing it to soften.

Connecting with the ground helps particularly when we are agitated, with the spine when we have lost direction, and with the belly and heart when we have lost touch with our feelings and become rather heady.

To make meditation easier

» Little and often is the best approach.

» When you bring awareness to your body in challenging situations it helps you to provide greater learning, perspective and creativity.

» Travelling is a really good time to pay attention to your body.

» Use time when you are waiting for someone else to develop greater awareness of yourself – even if it means being aware of how frustrations affect you.

» Develop a habit of punctuating your day with little periods of mindfulness, rather than simply rushing from one thing to another.

» The mind will always wander, that's what minds do. 'Success' in meditation is noticing that the mind has wandered and kindly, persistently, and patiently bringing it back to the object of concentration.

» Use as many support systems as you can find to develop a meditation practice: books, CDs, online tuition, and classes.

BUILD IN RECOVERY TIME

High performing athletes push themselves hard and then build in recovery time. Stage actors know that they need to rest in the mornings in order to perform at their best in the evening. An opera singer will spend less time performing on stage than she does looking after her voice, recovering after a performance or practising her repertoire at a quieter pace behind the scenes. Some professionals recognise that there's a high ratio of recovery to exertion time. How strange that this isn't the case in the workplace.

Applying the 80/20 rule is a good way to start to achieve a balance. That means aiming for 80 per cent recovery time for every 20 per cent that you're operating at your peak. As you raise your game, there's more recovery needed – a top athlete may need 95 per cent recovery.

When you are engrossed in any activity you're enjoying, or being pushed by external demands on you, you can stretch your physical energy levels beyond what's reasonable, especially when that entails travelling long haul across continents, as Philip found out.

Like an old kettle

After a recent trip, my colleague Philip, a management trainer, graphically told me how he arrived at Heathrow airport 'with the inside of my skull furred up like an old kettle, my mouth tasting like a bird cage, and every joint aching.' Thank goodness I didn't meet him that day!

He'd let himself get so low on energy that he was tempted to call the car breakdown service at the Automobile Association car recovery to plug his body into a battery charger. He'd been leaking power all week.

Six days earlier he had flown to an Asian city on a business trip. He flew through the night and lost a good night's sleep as well as 10 hours of time. The day after arriving, he delivered a 3-day workshop on his specialist topic to 12 very clever, well-educated people drawn from a range of countries in the Asia Pacific Region. They were very hospitable and wanted Philip to join them for all their meals and engage him in social conversation, so he gave himself no space for calm reflection.

He describes himself as having two tanks of energy – physical and emotional. 'I try to keep fit and look after myself but I knew that the physical one would start to drain as soon as I arrived at Heathrow for the outward bound flight.'

'Emotionally I lived off adrenalin as the workshop was going so well that it ignited the participants' curiosity. They were firing questions all the time which was exciting and kept me alert.'

He identifies five things that contributed to his extreme energy loss:

» *Sleeping in economy class for two nights on the plane.*

» *Facilitating a highly intensive workshop with clever people for three days.*

» *Socially conversing at every meal.*

» *Minimal time to switch off.*

» *Breathing air-conditioned air in all buildings and modes of transport.*

Boosting the batteries only began on his return to Heathrow when he walked through the airport instead of taking the moving walkway in order to mobilise his limbs, lungs and heart. 'And the taxi driver thought I was nuts, as I stuck my head out of the open window, breathing deeply.'

Once home, the first priority was a long shower, a large cup of Earl Grey tea and many glasses of water to help with rehydration. Then he tucked into porridge, with banana and blueberries, to get plenty of slow-burn carbohydrates. His ultimate booster was to stretch out between cool sheets for an early night, with windows open and fresh air to breathe.

Philip knows what he must do to recover, but next time he's vowed to pay more attention to the signals on his travels so that he doesn't experience a complete loss of energy.

Exercise

Boost your power

Physical energy can leak away rather like the charge in a car battery. To keep your power levels high, begin by identifying the leaks that sap your vitality. Think about how much time you may be spending on:

Trying to be in more than one
place at once .... minutes per week

Pleasing people at work .... minutes per week

Packing in too many activities .... minutes per week

Pleasing people at home	minutes per week
Worrying about requests for your time	minutes per week
Accepting unrealistic deadlines	minutes per week
Unnecessary travelling	minutes per week
Grabbing food on the run	minutes per week
Agonising over decisions	minutes per week
Listening to negative comments	minutes per week

All leaks will have an impact on your body. They lead to over-anxiety, over-tiredness and over-eating. To stem the leaks, increase the structures you have in place to enable you to conserve energy; without them, your power diffuses over a wide area and you are left tired. Get support as a priority and then use all the support you asked for.

Here are some further suggestions to tune into your physical energy and boost your power:

1. **Begin each day with intention.** Decide that you are going to pay attention to how healthily you approach the day. Look for the peak times that will tax you and see where you can add calm times.

2. **Check in with your body.** Notice where your body feels good or tense, and what that is telling you about food and nutrition. Have you drunk plenty of water? Do you need some fruit or seeds to give you a boost until the next meal? What is your body telling you about your emotional wellbeing?

3. **Find space in every day to indulge yourself a little.** When you are tired, you are less likely to step back, to witness what's happening and give yourself 10 minutes to celebrate and

rejuvenate. Take a walk or run, treat yourself to some delicious fruit, do a few stretches, play a favourite piece of music, light a scented candle.

4. **Do a daily energy check at the end of the day.**
Notice what made you feel physically good today and let this information inform the choices you make for how you spend tomorrow.

OPERATE BOUNDARY CONTROL

By sending out the message that you have set boundaries, you give yourself extra space between commitments. If you are always accessible to others, you lose valuable thinking time and the ability to live the life you really want for yourself. Boundary controls secure your physical energy as well as improving your control of time and money.

People pleasers take note here! If you love being with people and doing good for others, your physical energy will be depleted, unless you know how to say that small and under-used word 'no' or have a whole host of people around supporting you and picking up the load.

A coaching client recently suggested that he's 'rubbish' at setting boundaries; the invisible lines that separate his professional and personal life. He loves his work so much that the thought of stopping fills him with dread. When he was ill, he worked from his hospital bed, finding it gave him the energy to recover quickly from his illness. Another client told me that when she was ill, colleagues brought work to her in hospital, expecting papers to be read and decisions made even though she was seriously ill and wanted to be left alone to recover.

Some people function best with a clear demarcation between work and the rest of their lives; for others it's just one long gig enjoyed in the public eye. We each manage aspects of our life in our own way, just as some people like homes with several separate rooms while others prefer open plan living.

As a result of mobile technology, there is rarely a clear demarcation between our professional and personal lives. Whether your private time is spent with family, partner or special friends, it's getting interrupted. Boundary setting is a skill that involves conscious awareness of who we let into our lives, when and where, rather than being available to all people, all of the time.

So, when should work start and finish, particularly when you are engaged in what you do? I worked with somebody who loved to begin his working day between 5am and 6am every morning. By 8am he would want to call me to discuss projects and priorities. This doesn't fit with my best working style. Whenever possible, I reserve the start of the day for meditation time and exercise that boosts my energy to be with people for the rest of the day. Once I made this clear to him, we negotiated a way of working together that got the work done while playing to each of our strengths. He worked the morning shift as the 'lark' while I worked later in the day as the 'owl', happy to attend evening calls with colleagues in the US.

Where does the boundary lie?

In our physical environment we put up tangible boundaries – doors, walls, hedges, and fences to give privacy, security and separation from the rest of the world. In other aspects of our lives, we operate with the structure that boundaries provide:

» Switching telephones to voice mail or turning off computers.

» Fixing the start and end points of an appointment.

» Being available to other people – or not.

» Setting job descriptions which frame the work we will do, roles and responsibilities.

» Writing contracts that define the terms of engagement.

» Deciding which chores to take on at home or which to delegate.

» Having set meal times.

» Making 'family-only' time in parts of the day or weekend.

» Knowing our own strengths and when to refer people to others who can support them better.

In situations where you find a very flexible approach suits you best, your boundaries may be loosely defined while in areas that call for discipline and structure, you may find it more acceptable to have firm boundaries. There is no right or wrong way; just notice what works best for you. For example, if you find you've been very easy going and you find that somebody is taking liberties with your flexibility, ask yourself whether to exert tougher boundary control.

Louis Fischer's biography of Mahatma Gandhi, the leader responsible for India's independence, tells how much of Gandhi's life was lived in public view with a minimum of privacy, even to the point where he slept out in the open. By contrast, a Hollywood movie director and his actress wife told me how they cherish the time when they physically shut the door of their home on the outside world, to be with their family in an ordinary kind of way.

Boundaries clarify expectations, and provide punctuation marks in the dialogue of frazzled and disjointed lives. By shutting some doors, they open up a breathing space to give us the renewal time we need to stay healthy and energetic. They provide focus, privacy, structure, safety, and containment.

Life as a symphony

In his book *Like the Flowing River*, the Brazilian writer Paulo Coelho talks about the seasonality of his life and work with clear boundaries between each. He describes his life as a symphony composed of three distinct movements: 'a lot of people', 'a few people', and 'almost no one'. The 'a lot of people' time is when he's in touch with his public, publishers and journalists; the 'few people' moment is back home in Brazil where he mainly stays at home and accepts a few invitations to be with friends; and the 'almost no one' period occurs when he spends several months quietly hiding away in an isolated French farmhouse where he connects with the countryside and mountains. He says: 'I never think about who I am. I have no questions and no answers. I live entirely in the present moment.'

Such a pattern of four-month chunks might not be realistic for most of us with families and more conventional ways of earning a living, yet it can be repeated on a smaller scale so that our time 'out there' doing things is blended with the space to just live in the moment. Time-based events have clear boundaries: for example, limiting meetings and social engagements to a fixed start and finish time. It may be that you can create only short interludes for yourself in a crowded space like a train, plane or coffee shop. Even here you can create privacy by deliberately restricting access to yourself.

Create the golden cage around yourself

At times when you find yourself in difficult situations or you are mixing with people that you'd rather not be with, extra self-protection is required. So how can we achieve that without leaving the room? I have a friend who copes with the presence of plenty of very annoying people without appearing to get bothered about it. When I once asked him how he does that, he explained, 'In the back of my head, it's like a castle with a moat. The minute I feel someone getting to me, I pull up the drawbridge and go inside.'

In such situations, it can be helpful to visualise some kind of protective boundary to distance you from the pressures you experience as the following exercise shows.

Thought provoker

Imagine that you have a finely-crafted wonderful golden structure to protect you, a delicate framework that you can step in and out of and where no one can touch you. You and only you hold the key to this cage. As you move in, you are a free animal or bird, one who has chosen to be there for your own safety and protection from the ravages of the outside world.

Like a beautiful creature with all your delicate features and finery, this structure around you is so light and airy that you can travel wherever you wish in the knowledge that you are separate and secure from any fear of danger. The boundary is clear; you are untouchable.

Consider for a moment where you might travel with this golden cage around you in your mind's eye. You can time travel back into the past to revisit early experiences to gain additional insights or into the future to explore new possibilities.

Who would you approach with this invisible protection? What impossible dreams become possible with the knowledge that you can land safely wherever you choose?

DISCONNECT THE DRAINERS

Certain people in your life would drain your energy if you allowed them to. Maybe you have a relative who finds life difficult and wants to offload their troubles onto you when you already have enough of your own, or a friend who likes to bemoan his lack of success in dating the perfect girl? Perhaps you're tempted to be the world's most helpful person, willing to rescue others and constantly coming up with ways that you can solve their issues? Giving too generously with your time can mean time you are not investing in your own healthy routines, so leaving you in poorer health.

For example: At work – are you working on projects with people who leave you feeling low in energy, exhausted to the point that you are like a damp tea towel, no good even for drying dishes at the end of the day? This doesn't mean that they are inherently bad people, just that they are motivated by different things and work in a very different way to you. Such people are encountered every day. Over time they are a health hazard. There's a fine line between accepting somebody's idiosyncrasies and being drained by them.

Top tip

List five people who make you feel energised and make a note in your diary to spend more time with them.

Jez is a civil servant and told me how the director he worked for thrived on complexity which was exhausting. The minute that those around the director had solved one problem, she would come up with dozens more, bringing in sophisticated models and theories. 'When we thought a task was complete, she would continually go back and change the parameters, asking for everything to be re-worked.'

The director couldn't allow anything to be straightforward or simple because, unless she could make a change, she didn't feel she had contributed anything of value. She seemed to love having staff buzzing around in circles, oblivious to the fact that several of her key managers had gone off sick with stress-related illnesses. Jez had got to the point where he was seriously considering leaving the public sector and shifting into a commercial enterprise.

When he looked for a new posting, he was offered three opportunities in different government departments. This time, before he accepted a new role, he asked to shadow his potential bosses for a day. He made an informed choice to switch to an office where he felt he could work more independently and be trusted to make decisions. 'It's proved to be a healthier option for me.'

The elegant disconnect

When you recognise that a situation is toxic, it's time to pull the plug and redirect your focus. You can do this politely and respectfully without upsetting anyone.

How? On the work front you may need to distance yourself from a colleague by avoiding meetings and communication with them, even shifting to a different department or role if the situation is particularly bad. On the social front, try moving in new circles – going to different clubs, trying different activities. Gently release anything or anybody who consistently drains you and you'll be saving large amounts of personal energy.

As a hypnotherapist, Jon works with people with weight issues. He told me of one new client, Sandra, who arrived in his practice room and said: 'Just hypnotise me to eat less, will you?' 'Before I do that, can you just tell me what you ate yesterday?' he asked. On hearing the list of high sugar foods, he pointed out that she needed to take responsibility for changing her diet as well as her thoughts about food. She grimaced at the idea of actually making any changes herself and he never heard from her again.

From Jon's point of view, the fact that this client never came back proved to be a good move. It's never healthy to work with clients who sap your energy because they want to put the burden of responsibility for success on anybody but themselves.

Many self-employed people and business owners persist in working with clients who are quick to blame their suppliers.

If you are in business, remember that it's better to let some clients go if they are not a good fit for how you work. If you work in an organisation for a manager who bullies or belittles you, it's time to polish your CV and get out before your own self-esteem hits the floor.

You might be thinking that this is unrealistic: 'That's all very well, I have to stick this job/work with this client/ I have rent to pay and food to buy.' The reality is that unhappy business relationships will take their toll on your health. There's a decision to be made if it's worth the effort to change the dynamic. If you were married to that person, my advice would be different as you have (hopefully) had a loving relationship with that person as the foundation, and you'd want to make some effort before moving on. In the workplace, we meet people who we do not match with; their values and behaviour are so different that it's better to realise that we can't work well with everyone, and politely move on.

CREATE NEW RITUALS

In paying attention to our wellbeing, we send out a clear message that we will no longer tolerate second best for our bodies. In this chapter, we've looked at ways to increase physical energy including:

» Setting stronger boundaries
» Getting your body in the best possible physical shape
» Paying attention to the effects of diet, caffeine and addictive substances
» Protecting yourself from others' demands

However healthy we consider ourselves to be, there will be days, weeks and months where what we do saps our bodies. Elements of our work will tax us physically, with long days out working, travelling on buses, planes, trains, nipping up motorways in a hurry, sorting paperwork, using technology, managing accounts and writing documents to deadlines. Life outside work can also be physically demanding as any parent with small children knows. Beyond family life there will be activities with friends, sports and hobbies to fill the diary. How easy to overlook the basic chores that take energy. We need to buy and prepare food, make sure we have clean clothes and a welcoming living environment. Nothing changes unless we do something different.

Exercise

New daily habits

Now's the time to consider some new things you want to do for yourself that will secure the foundation for your health for the long term. Be creative, find things that energise and motivate you. Find those things that can become rituals for the 21 days until the habit is embedded. Make a note of them on the chart and tick off each day to remind you of the habit.

For example:

- » Plan each day's healthy meals.
- » Finish work by 6pm.
- » Drink eight glasses of water each day.
- » Have a piece of fruit for mid-morning and mid-afternoon snacks.

» Choose a new food or recipe to try instead of the same old ones.

» Enjoy quiet time before going to bed.

» Have an alcohol-free day.

» Get eight hours sleep.

» Limit TV viewing to weekends.

» Exercise for 15 minutes a day.

» Practice a new sport.

» Take a 20-minute relaxation slot for every 80 minutes of work.

When you have a good long list of habits you'd like to introduce, pick out your top three and work on these for the next three weeks. Once these are firmly embedded, choose another three to build up. Copy the chart and put it somewhere like the kitchen or bathroom where you'll see it every day and can tick off your new habits.

Build in a reward for yourself for keeping to your new habits. Choose something healthy and have fun!

Daily Habits

New Habit	1	2	3	4	5	6	7	8	9	10	11	12	13	14	15	16	17	18	19	20	21
Drink water																					

CHAPTER **3**

MENTAL ENERGY

Your Wonderful Mind

Accept the Adventure

168 Hours to Spend

Focus on Your Strengths

Pay Attention to Signals

Find the Extreme Hobby

To live satisfying lives with rewarding work, we need the ability to stay mentally stimulated and alert without tipping into anxiety, boredom or becoming overwhelmed. To keep our thoughts on track is easier said than done. In this chapter we'll be concentrating on the part that our intellect plays in the equation.

Mental energy is about staying resilient in the face of adversity and the challenges that life and the workplace bring: being stimulated and interested in what we are doing; building on our natural strengths and focusing our time on the things that are most important for us. Just as we preserve our physical energy through a good diet and exercise, so our mental energy needs stretching, relaxation and a strong mindset.

Just pause for a moment to consider a difficulty or surprise you have had in your life that has translated into an opportunity. Maybe you've had bad news? Maybe you've learnt something about yourself that came as a shock to hear? Maybe you've been embarrassed by a mistake you made? What one good thing, however small, came out of your experience?

You naturally have the human skills to learn from experiences and direct your thought process to your advantage. The aim is to boost this mental skill further to create an easy state of flow where all of your mental faculties are harnessed and work to your best advantage.

In his work, *The Psychology of Optimal Experience*, Mihaly Csikszentmihalyi explored the state of flow that people experience when they are operating at their mental best.

Often we recognise flow more by its absence than its presence. When we face a challenge that seems higher than our skill level, we experience anxiety. When our skill levels are much higher than the challenge, we experience boredom. The flow state is the mental route between the two: this is the place to be, most of the time.

Think of a time when you were fully absorbed in what you were doing, so the time just flew. You were alert, everything felt effortless, and you were unselfconscious. You were just having a ball. This is what we mean by a 'state of flow'.

» When the challenge is much higher than the skill, we experience anxiety
» When the skill is much higher than the challenge, we experience boredom
» The flow channel lies between anxiety and boredom

Flow states allow us to perform at our best in work and enjoy the greatest quality of life beyond our work. How, then, can we achieve this ease of flow more of the time?

» Identifying environments where we thrive – being with the right people, in places that suit us.

» By doing the things that fit right for us.

» Developing and using all our skills while continuing to learn.

» By operating in line with our values, the factors that are important to us.

» Enjoying a sense of identity where 'it's OK to be me'.

» Engaging in purposeful activity where we're achieving something that fits just right for us.

Exercise

Working in flow

In order to find work that really sings to your soul, look back to a time when you were working in a flow state – content, energised and focused. It may have been one day; it may have been a period of weeks, months or years. Capture your answers to the following questions:

Where was I and who was I with, what kind of place was it?

....

....

What work was I doing?

....

....

Which of my skills was I using? What was I learning?

....

....

What was important to me?

....

....

What was my sense of self at that time? How did I feel about my role
and how that fitted me?

....

....

How did what I was doing make a difference for others?

....

....

Now repeat the exercise with two other positive work experiences.
Once you have considered all three experiences, draw up a check-
list of what needs to be in place for you to work at your best. Keep
it on a card or a page in your diary so that when any opportunities
come up you can check for yourself that it's the best possible fit
for you.

YOUR WONDERFUL MIND

The human mind is made up of a wonderful complexity of
conscious and unconscious components. In the flow state, our
mental energy is all lined up – the conscious and unconscious

mind working together without interference. We are being ourselves and doing what we do at our best.

The conscious mind is often likened to the tip of an iceberg visible above an icy ocean. This conscious space holds short-term memory and the ability to analyse current activity in the moment. Below the surface of the water, the unconscious mind is a massive storehouse of memories and information beavering away to take care of your body and drive your emotions.

Most business work encourages us to think very logically, driven by performance measures and deadlines. It occupies the conscious mind and overlooks the power and creativity in the unconscious mind. It's worth remembering that the unconscious mind is benevolent, with your best interests at heart. This is why we lie awake at night with the mind all over the place when something in life is not working out as we wish. The unconscious is helping us to grapple with the dilemma and move to a resolution.

Our thoughts stimulate our actions, which in turn create the experiences that make up our life. That is why it always helps to harness great thoughts! When we recognise the effect that the quality of our thinking has on our lives, then we increase our power to live the life we want. When we are dissatisfied or unhappy there is a tendency to focus solely on the negative aspects of our work or life. By switching the focus of attention from dwelling on problems to identifying what it is we want – the outcomes – we have the greatest chance to affect the result.

One simple way to do this is by setting your intent about how you are going to behave. For example, as you start your day, you decide you're going to notice all the good things that have happened to you instead of the bad. You choose how you will behave as you walk into a room full of strangers – whether nervous or inquisitive. When you set your intent, you are defining your state of mind; you are choosing how you want to be, regardless of what needs to be done or how anybody else around you behaves. You steer your own journey. You also bring your unconscious mind along for the ride.

The conscious and unconscious mind function in unison when we set clear goals about what we want to achieve, and understand our sense of values and purpose. We'll be exploring more about this in Chapter 5 on purposeful energy. Without this clarity, unconscious fears will muscle in to steer us in the wrong direction.

ACCEPT THE ADVENTURE

Life is an adventure and, like all good movies, features villains as well as heroes, surprises as well as predictable action. You can set a strong direction about how you would like life to turn out with goals in place that map all the things you'd like to do. However, it would be very dull to know at the outset how it would end and not enjoy the spontaneity of the journey and allow your heart to have its place as well as the logical mind.

It will never be possible to be fully in control of every aspect of your life. Setting your intent to accept life as an adventure rather than worrying about controlling every detail will lead to it becoming a more enjoyable experience and strengthen your mental capacity to deal with whatever life throws in your path, both in work and your personal life.

When we embrace adventures of any kind, we are bombarded with new information, meeting new people and situations and gaining a broader perspective. Each fresh episode challenges our preconceived mental patterns about 'this is the way things always are' because we see that there are exceptions to our rules. From creating new ways of thinking, we create new ways of behaving.

Just as nature has its seasons – times to plant, weed and nurture, times to harvest what's been sown – our thought patterns shift through a seasonality of their own. At times it's best to discard old ways of thinking, cutting back those ideas and assumptions which no longer serve us and being open to enjoy new ones.

Seeing the choices

Shifting to a point of acceptance enables us to move on, sow new seeds and flourish in a different way. Time and time again, you will need to be resilient to change – however painful it feels at the time.

Until you get to the point of truly accepting what is happening, you will feel the resistance as you battle against it. You may waver backwards and forwards, through periods of one minute accepting and then another resisting anxiously what is happening until you re-connect with your creativity once more and move into purposeful action.

When Mark was told that his department was relocating to a business park 30 miles away on the outskirts of the city, he was very concerned about how he would build the travelling time into his day. He had chosen this job because it enabled him to take his children to the local school each morning and get to the gym in his lunch break. He spent hours at the coffee machine denouncing, 'This is not fair', then went home every night making malicious comments about the management team to his wife.

His colleagues began to feel worn down by his moaning and resentful attitude as he fell behind on his work. Most began to avoid him until one piped up: 'You've two choices, Mark. Get on with it or get out.' Only then did he negotiate with his manager to work flexible hours and organise new childcare arrangements with his wife.

After the 9 to 5

When a major change to our working lives takes place, like redundancy, it's tempting to accept the first new job opportunity that presents itself as a safety net. Once the glint of a new job or business proposition wears off, unless the work is a true match to our selection criteria, we are setting ourselves up to fail. Allow time for a period of thoughtful consideration (revisiting the 'Working in flow' exercise regularly) and experimention as part of the adventure of change.

Martin, an oil company executive, had been with his company for 29 years and had recently accepted a new post in the UK after a successful posting overseas. But for the past six months things hadn't been going well at work. He liked to be kept busy, but the job was not keeping him occupied. He found himself increasingly criticised by his manager and was eventually told his job was 'at risk'. This placed him on the redundancy list.

'I had been so focused on getting back into the UK that I chose a job quickly that seemed a good fit.' Martin had ignored the finer details of the job specification.

When redundancy hit, Martin found himself angry and stressed. 'My anger was not just about being made redundant, but also the way it was done. I felt that I was thrown on the heap; as if I was useless.'

The impact of redundancy is complex. Early retirement with a comfortable pension and time to play golf left him the envy of other hardworking colleagues. Yet in situations like this, we lose our sense of identity. The purpose and structure to our lives takes time and investigation to replace. Who are you when you can no longer answer the question, 'What do you do?'

Rejection in Martin's mind turned in time to acceptance and then relief as he noticed, 'It was actually a pretty good opportunity.'

Throughout his career Martin felt he had a sound mix of home and work life. Having a stable and loving home to come back to was the reason for going out to work. When back in London, he'd work regular hours and leave work in the office. When jobs came up where he knew he'd have to work very long hours, he didn't apply. Instead he took the interesting ones. 'I looked for challenging projects that enabled me to travel and work with different people.'

Martin is now relishing the change to self-employment as he lets go of anxiety about future roles. 'It would have been a bold choice for me to throw in the security, but with hindsight I've seen that interesting work beyond the company was possible to find and very enjoyable.' He now feels that he has regained the mental challenge on which he thrives.

Finding the good

You may have heard the story of the king in Africa whose close friend had a habit of looking at every situation that ever occurred in his life (positive or negative) and remarking, 'This is good.'

The story goes like this...

> One day the king and his friend were out on a hunting expedition and the friend loaded the guns for the king. Something went wrong in preparing one of the guns, for after taking the gun from his friend, the king fired it and blew his own thumb off.
>
> Examining the situation, the friend remarked as usual: 'This is good!' To which the king sent his friend to jail, replying: 'No, this is NOT good!'
>
> About a year later, the king was hunting in an area that he should have known to stay clear of. Cannibals captured him and took him to their village. They tied his hands, stacked some wood, set up a stake and bound him to it. As they came near to set fire to the wood, they noticed that the king was missing a thumb.
>
> Being superstitious, they never ate anyone who was less than whole. So, untying the king, they sent him on his way.
>
> As the king returned home, he was reminded of the hunting event that had taken his thumb and felt remorse for his treatment of his friend. He went immediately to the jail to speak with his friend.

'You were right,' he said, 'it was good that my thumb was blown off.' And he proceeded to tell the friend all that had just happened. 'And so I am very sorry for sending you to jail for so long. It was bad for me to do this.'

'No,' his friend replied, 'This is good!' To which the king answered: 'What do you mean, "This is good"? How could it be good that I sent my friend to jail for a year?'

'If I had NOT been in jail, I would have been with you.'

The friend demonstrates his innate mental resilience, turning each disaster into a positive ending.

Building self-confidence

When I run 'Confidence in Adversity' workshops, I remind participants that personal freedom begins with understanding and accepting ourselves as we are. Our self-confidence can grow dramatically when we go through tough times if we accept each failure or misfortune as an opportunity to learn and develop our resilience.

When times are tough, those who are able to think in a flexible way will gradually let go of the past. Those who try to hold on to the injustice or wish things to be other than they are will prolong their mental anguish and take longer to transform their situation. I don't mean that you should deny that a situation is horrible when it is; but that you focus on developing a strong survivor's mindset – seeing beyond the present day.

Your personal confidence grows as you develop your ability to take appropriate and effective action regardless of how you feel inside. Remember that it's putting your thoughts into action that transforms situations. A positive mindset alone leaves you in the same position.

The way through

As a Contracts Manager Joan loved the mental buzz of contract negoti-ation and managing people. She was determined to keep that skill alive when she left the corporate world to pursue her love of art, travel and walking. The mental toughness she developed now serves her well. For ten years, she has led walking holidays all over the world, experiencing amazing scenery and meeting new people while staying superbly fit.

Joan feels that her comfort with her lifestyle comes down to concen-trating on a few things that are important to her. She looks after her health, stays in touch with a handful of good friends, can live simply and likes to add value to others' travel experiences. 'I don't expect to be happy all the time, I am just content,' she says.

As a female leader, she's faced some tricky situations. She was mugged in Ecuador and robbed in France. Once she had to get a lady who suffered a heart attack from a remote mountain top in Turkey to a hospital 80 miles away while being responsible for the safety of the other walkers.

She also talks of many magical moments: of sunsets in the Grand Canyon, of the hidden quarters of Marrakesh and the treasures of India.

She sees each situation as a mini puzzle to solve, with step-by-step choices and decision points, refusing to allow herself to get caught up in the anxiety of keeping 20 people happy each day. She feels that all her early business experience stands her in good stead. 'I just go with what happens and work it out,' she says. 'There's always a way through.'

Surprises into opportunities

As a coach, I'm privileged to bear witness to my clients' lives – and often we meet when life has seemingly gone pear-shaped. People talk about the loss of a job, bereavement, a disastrous relationship, the terrible behaviour of a boss, child, spouse or parent. There may be a presentation, interview or date that has gone badly. In my experience, with a change in focus, some good does eventually comes out of the tough situations. People discover their motivation to head off and do new things and the resilience to get up and try again as they create new lives.

Small things pick us up when we go through tough times. One October, on a close friend's death in Holland, I consoled myself by choosing many packs of tulip bulbs to plant which would flower the following spring. One particular variety proved to be stunning and each October I plant dozens of them and give packs to other gardening friends. As they bloom, not only do I re-connect with my friend's wonderful spirit, but others get tremendous pleasure from seeing the tulips in full flower.

Stroppy or what?

Chris runs a customer training centre and is an advocate for keeping mentally alert, challenging your own assumptions and considering other points of view as you go about your daily business. One morning he was asked to assist a young trainer faced with a 'highly stroppy' student – a middle-aged manager. The man was disrupting the class, asking strange questions and not doing the exercises that the trainer had set.

Chris marched into the training centre to sort the problem, ready to evict the troublemaker. When he asked if he could have a word with the student, the training centre receptionist replied: 'Only after the ambulance crew has finished with him.'

It emerged that the student in question was diabetic and in need of insulin. He was not being intentionally disruptive. The training staff were left feeling very embarrassed that they had misread the signals.

The upside of the incident is that Chris now uses his 'embarrassing moment' to illustrate his talks on workplace health and safety.

There is usually an upside in even the most dire situation. Few people who've been made redundant have regrets about it later in their careers. Those whose relationships have failed eventually see that it happened for a reason. An unexpected pregnancy or illness can create the space to think differently about priorities, offering the chance to live life in a new way. In retrospect, the response to personal challenge is usually: 'It was tough at the time, yet it gave me the jolt I needed to do something different.'

Top tip

If you lose your job, there's no point in spending all day and night worrying and job hunting. Head for a day at the beach, take time to play as well as pursuing the job applications. Live in the moment and have fun. Recognise this time as a breathing space giving you more freedom to do things during the day that you wouldn't have considered before. Start writing your novel, dabble in paint, sing, dance, make music, decorate your home. Few people working hard say that they have too much play time.

168 HOURS TO SPEND

"Things which matter most must never be at the mercy of things which matter least."

Goethe

With just 168 hours of time in your diary to spend each week, budgeting wisely requires logical thinking and decision-making so that you feel satisfied with your purchases. Practical planning keeps the mental energy flowing as you stay on track to concentrate on the most important things in your life.

Hanging in the window of my office is an ornamental star-fish made of wood, with a rope of golden coins, a surprise gift from friends who came on a writers' retreat that I led on a Greek island. It's a gentle reminder that time is like these special coins, a resource to spend wisely. Each moment is precious; there is no reliving the past except in our memories and photographs; no reset button allowing you to turn the clock back to that younger you. Life is short. Once spent, you will not be able to recapture exactly the same coins.

Like loose change abandoned on the floor from trouser pockets, time builds into bigger notes. Weeks, months, years and decades can pass until you wake up to your own life and wonder just how you have spent it. If we're really to live the life we love, then it's helpful to tune into our spending patterns, especially to choose purposefully about the tiny moments, because each drop counts.

The formula for the 168-hour spending pattern is simple; the implementation may be more challenging and require conscious determination and support along the way.

Step 1 **Set Your Priorities** – know where you are going, your goals, dreams and what's important to you.

Step 2 **Formulate a Plan** – with steps along the way and resources to help you.

Step 3 **Take Action** – take the first step and then the next one without getting side-tracked.

Step 4 **Review** – check the results you are getting, go back to the plan and adapt as necessary.

Exercise

How do you really spend your life?

Consider your life as like a bank account using the blank time bank account sheet below as your template. Here's how it works:

» You begin with a set income of 168 hours in a week.

» Indentify the regular payments you make, the standing orders and direct debits of time. i.e. how many hours do you give to work, your family, your friends, your hobbies, your sleep?

» Make a note of how you are actually spending your time, the key things you are voting for.

» Consider whether how you actually spend your time compares with your dreams and aspirations. Are you making conscious, deliberate choices based on your real priorities?

» Decide which area to focus on to make time savings. (Television is a tremendous time-stealer.) Don't choose to cut back on sleep. You need it!

» Identify the first steps to move you along the way.

The time bank account

Activities Choose a typical working week	Current reality HOURS	Future goal HOURS	Simplify What one action can you take to release time?
Work (list five key areas of your work role – e.g. key projects, client-facing work, admin and calls, accounts/budgets, training, planning, team leading, reporting, communications)			
Commuting time			
Home			
Time with partner/family			
Hobbies/sport/friends			
Domestic chores			
Relaxation and self-care			
Sleep			
TOTAL	*168*	*168*	

Ready for action

'When I experience myself exactly as I am, I change,' said the therapist Carl Rogers. As you know more about yourself and realise how you are spending your time, you cannot help but make changes.

Julie, a 32-year old sales executive in a pharmaceutical company, has invested the last 10 years in her career. She's spent her hard-earned cash on a wardrobe full of executive clothes: neat skirts, jackets and shirts, smart briefcases, designer watches and scarves. This single-minded investment has left other parts of her life starving hungry. Recently, she's woken up to feeling lonely, shy and terrified of social engagements. She's angry at herself, disillusioned by being swallowed up by the choices she's made. By skewing her time expenditure on the work front, she feels at a loss within herself.

There's a part of Julie that is desperate to escape from work, to bury her head in the sand, abandoning time debts because she's frustrated with what she considers to be her wasted years. To add to the pressure, her 'biological baby clock' is also ticking furiously: she's hoping like crazy that her male hero, the knight on the white charger, will arrive to carry her off to a safe place where she can concentrate on the feminine side of her life, being wife and mother, believing that her life will then be truly wonderful.

To begin to redress this situation, she is looking at the time equation intently. Now she's ready to be master of her own time she is setting new plans in place to release time for friends and new interests that will allow the space for romance to happen.

Be master of your time

As we practise mastering our time, we send a message to those around us about how we value ourselves. If you set yourself up to please everyone all of the time, you'll end up pleasing nobody. You will never have enough hours in the day to do all that you could do for everyone. Accept that some people are just going to be disappointed that they can't get enough of you.

Quit wasting the minutes

Notice the little bits of extra time you give away and begin to monitor your time. When you overrun a meeting by ten minutes, you are losing ten minutes that you could spend elsewhere – at home with your loved one, practising your trumpet, supporting your favourite team, getting fitter, or out in the world aligned with your favourite cause. Clean up on time wasters – block out unwanted sales callers or moaning colleagues; prepare ahead for meetings so that less time is spent on peripheral discussions; limit the time you spend on newspapers, junk mail, TV and surfing the net.

Buy yourself thinking time

When a request for your time, money or energy comes at you, give yourself a while to consider before saying 'yes'. Instead say: 'I'll come back to you.' Remember that time and money are connected. Everything you spend money on is ultimately paid for in terms of the hours you work.

Regular stock takes

At frequent intervals, re-evaluate how much is spent on:

» **Panics and problems** – those important deadline-driven jobs that need to be sorted quickly.

» **Plans and longer-term opportunities** – important, longer-term projects including relationship building. Aim to spend your time in this space.

» **Pressing items** – ones that may not be important on your priority list, even though someone is pushing you to do them.

» **'Pootling' time** – like chats and trivia at the coffee shop and email jokes.

Block out 'me time'

Create 'me time' in your schedule – areas of time where there's no schedule to 'do' anything, you can just 'be' for a change, where you give yourself pure down time. Have you noticed how the best ideas emerge when you're in the shower and thinking of nothing in particular?

In the same way, when you give yourself space to just be in the moment, you allow your natural creativity to come through. Blocking out this 'me time' may be the toughest challenge you face. Surprising as it sounds, these pockets of time will actually give you more time in the longer run.

Get radical

» Consider how you give yourself time to wake up in the morning to be in the best possible 'state'. Do you rush out of bed late, or build exercise in to the early hours of your day and clear yourself some uninterrupted thinking time? Starting the day on our own terms gives us a greater sense of being grounded later, as others' demands fly in.

» Turn your day upside down so that you begin with important and not urgent projects and bite away at them, rather than always devoting mental energy to troubleshooting problems.

» Ignore post and messages until later than usual. Quit responding as fast as a Pavlovian dog to every stimulus, and question just how much of your email is really necessary. Choose those circulation lists that you wish to be on and ask senders to delete you from the rest.

FOCUS ON YOUR STRENGTHS

When you do something effortlessly, you step into the state of 'flow' that we discussed at the start of the chapter. However, we become blind to our own expertise. This is why it's useful to get feedback from others. We all need mentors, coaches, teachers, friends and supportive family to help us recognise the strengths that we so easily overlook.

Exercise

The talent list

Take a piece of paper. List all the life skills you can think of that you possess. What are you especially good at? What are the strong aspects of your personality? Think of every single context of your life. Are you friendly? Optimistic? Do you organise people well? Are you tidy? Creative? Do you have big ideas?

Start writing a list and keep going until you reach the bottom of the page. Invite friendly feedback from family, colleagues and mentors about the special talents that you've overlooked.

Now ask yourself which of your talents you'd like to make more of in your professional and personal life. Look back at your 168 hours and see whether you are allocating time to activities that fit with your talents, and if not, make this a priority.

As you adjust your life to encompass the things you are good at, you'll experience a greater sense of flow and learn to recognise the early warning signs that tell you when things aren't going so well. In time, you will stop battling to be someone you aren't and will make life easier for yourself.

Outsourced feelings

Like many 40-something-year-old professionals, Anna believed that her work life was 'a mug's game'. Despite holding a prestigious directorship in a firm of management consultants, her everyday reality was a job where her ideas were not listened to and a situation in which she was feeling increasingly powerless to do a good job for her clients.

Crunch time came while trying to access the company intranet from home at 7am one Saturday morning after a 58-hour working week. Anna realised she was physically and emotionally exhausted. She felt she was 'Piggy in the middle: working on a bid that I knew would fail and targets that were not achievable.' In spite of being in line for a company partnership, the role did not match her values and could not satisfy her intellectually.

Anna chose to jump from her lucrative career track and she shifted to a smaller consultancy instead, where she would earn less, use her skills and learn more. That proved to be the stepping stone to setting up her own business.

'I needed to get away from a culture where the only measure of success and value was sales. Human needs always had to be subordinate and discounted,' she says. 'Of course, I still have sales targets, but my

business planning is now driven by focusing on the ways I can add value to clients.'

Today she still works in tough environments, often doing paperwork at weekends, yet she finds real joy in honing her skills and creativity and being in partnership with her clients. 'Now I have a lot of career highs each year, with very few lows.'

Saying 'yes' and saying 'no'

You will need to let go of those things that are not working to create space for new things that will work. Yet to achieve this takes constant focus. Think of letting go of past behaviours as a cathartic declutter. The yes/no list approach described below is for all those times when you feel you are riding the rollercoaster, becoming overwhelmed and losing your state of flow.

The key question to ask is: 'Am I doing the things that only I can do?'

Exercise

Yes/no lists

» Take a piece of paper and draw a vertical line down the middle to create two columns. Add two headings with 'yes' at the head of one column and 'no' at the top of the other.

» In each column write down things that you are saying yes and no to in your life and work. Your focus could be a very specific area such as 'volunteer activities' or 'requests from my family'. It could be a habitual way of being.

» Step back to see what are you saying 'yes' to that you'd prefer to say 'no' to. Are you saying 'yes' to things that take your energy or give you more? When you say 'yes' to the 'wrong' things, it means you'll be saying 'no' to what your heart truly desires.

» Now list some of the tasks, people, thoughts and situations that you need to let go of in order to boost your energy and keep you connected to your core.

» Set yourself a timeframe by when each of these will happen and think about who would be willing to help you make this happen.

By consistently refining your choices in this way, you conserve your mental energy for the most important things.

PAY ATTENTION TO SIGNALS

Overwhelm with work or other life commitments can build quietly and take us by surprise unless we make a mental note to regularly check what is happening. Some years ago I was told the story of Nan-in, a Japanese master who received a university professor who came to inquire about Zen. It goes like this:

Nan-in poured the tea. He poured his visitor's cup full and then kept on pouring.

The professor watched the cup overflow until he could no longer restrain himself. 'It is over-full. No more will go in.'

'Like this cup,' Nan-in said, 'you are full of your own opinions and speculations. How can I show you Zen unless you first empty your cup?'

Like the professor's cup in the Zen story, our brains get flooded with ideas to the point that we can't focus on the truth of what is really happening in front of our eyes. This 'busyness' of adding more and more activity into our lives can become addictive and counter-productive.

Avoidance games

Busyness can itself be an unconscious distraction from underlying fears that we don't want to consciously think about. We all play avoidance games when there's something to be done or said that we don't find comfortable. As a writer, I'll confess my ability to load the washing machine, fiddle with software, tidy my desk, phone a friend – a million and one little devices to avoid facing the scary blank page.

Some avoidance strategies result in getting no work done at all. At other times, work becomes fully engrossing to the exclusion of priorities in the outside world. Often we don't articulate what we're avoiding until we become aware of our own little games.

Through his 20s and early 30s, IT consultant Raz had got into the habit of staying late and going into the office at weekends; it was better than being at home alone in his flat or visiting his mother and stepfather whom he disliked intensely. Whenever his mother called, he curtailed the conversation with: 'Can't stop now, Mum. We've got system issues.' Or, 'Sorry, have to work this weekend. Real problems with a customer in the city.'

Work became a way of covering up his increasing loneliness and also exacerbated the situation. By the time he did take holidays or weekends off, he was too tired to enjoy them. 'I remember one ski holiday in the Alps where I spent the first three days sleeping as I was so exhausted,' he said. 'I missed out on the ski lessons that everyone else had booked, and got left behind on the skiing, so I ended up checking my email in the chalet alone.'

More and more of his friends were shifting from single to married life, so the band of old friends that he could rely on to go out with dwindled to nothing.

'I was very good at filling my time with work. I was the one who could always be relied on to do the jobs that involved travelling or anti-social hours, so I made myself very useful.'

Change only happened thanks to a reorganisation and the arrival of a new IT director. When Ruth came on the scene, she said she had a policy of deliberately chucking people out of the office. She wanted her people working smart, not long. 'After all, why aren't we making the technology work for us instead of the other way around?' was her view.

Raz told me that he felt very uncomfortable with a new policy that his colleagues loved. No longer was he going to be appreciated for staying at work. 'In the past, I had earned "brownie points" for being first in and last out of the office. Now I was told that the boss wanted "alive and engaged people who were well-rounded individuals", and she wouldn't appreciate receiving late night emails from me.'

With more time on his hands, Raz very reluctantly accepted an invitation to a local tango dancing class with some married friends. They told him that men were in short supply and he was needed. Raz found that he loved the music and the mental challenge of remembering the dance steps. It opened up a world of Saturday night dances up and down the country and a new network of friends.

By deliberately chucking Raz out of the office, his new boss had done him a huge favour in helping him to have a whole life. He also brought a fresh approach to work on Monday mornings; he had more interesting conversations and was more appealing to his colleagues. This, in *turn, led to him dating a girl from work that he'd been too shy to invite out.*

Access your dreams

We think that we make clear decisions when we have multiple facts to hand. The truth is that we limit our mental powers when only thinking logically. The best decisions are made when we call on our unconscious brain to help us.

Dreams, meditation and relaxation techniques all enable us to get centred, back to a core place for calm decision-making where we can access the power of the unconscious. Dreams, in particular, are an untapped source to engage our creativity and open up new ideas.

If we want to dream more, we need to cultivate good sleeping habits. Instead of working right up to bedtime on the computer, watching TV or talking with friends, it helps to allow more 'down time' – another half an hour to relax and quieten down your thoughts. Cutting out stimulants like caffeine and alcohol also makes a difference.

Leading scientists such as Descartes and Einstein attributed their breakthroughs to their ability to dream. As we process our dreams, the insights we gain can help us to solve any problem. If you have a dilemma that you're trying to solve, before going to sleep invite your unconscious mind to provide you with solutions as you sleep. Simply say to yourself before you go to sleep: 'Please help me with …' naming the issue you're struggling with. Then, in the morning as you wake, stay in bed a extra few minutes to recall dreams or thoughts about your issue.

Psychologists suggest that only 20 per cent of our dreams have a positive emotional tone. Even scary dreams act as a reminder of the deep concerns worth heeding and offer a space to explore and to respond through the mechanism of the dream.

Exercise

Dream book

Remembering and recording dreams is a way to clear your head to start the day, and to provide a rich source of ideas. Keep a notebook by your bed to record your dreams immediately on waking. Notice the characters, the situations and symbols that recur – bring these to your attention into your waking moments and look for the connection between the dream and any challenges you face. What advice have your dreams got for you? What are the qualities of the symbol that can be useful for you?

FIND THE EXTREME HOBBY

Revisit the allocation of time in your 168 hours exercise and consider how much time there is in your life for hobbies and relaxation. Most people who do this exercise find that the spare time in their schedules is miniscule. The fun time and moments of escape get squeezed out when we are busy.

When a friend invited me to a workshop on comic improvisation, I went along with some apprehension. It felt like an indulgence of time and a chance to be made to look foolish with a group of strangers. Instead, I laughed so much that my stomach ached. I left behind all my worries completely and even now giggle to think about the day. Extreme hobbies change our mental chemistry which in turn affects all aspects of our energy.

Too much conscious thought can be draining. By trying to be logical and maintain control we lose the ability to just 'be' in the moment. Finding a hobby that is out of the ordinary, or doing something very different at work, will boost your mental energy, giving you a complete mind break from the regular day.

Fellow coach Angela told me that she used to relax by making models from salt dough. Every evening, she'd come home from her job in PR for an electronics company and mould a new creation to bake in the oven until the house was full of weird and wonderful characters and shapes. Sometimes she was so involved in the model making that she'd get up in the middle of the night to bake her creations. Now she's turned her attention to writing poems as a way to switch off into a creative mode – the poems take up less space!

You may already enjoy a range of activities like swimming or gardening that give you a welcome break. Consider adding to your repertoire something completely different, that stretches your mental faculties in a new direction.

Choose an activity that defies you to tap into your Blackberry or PC, somewhere that you will not even think about turning it on. From sci-fi appreciation societies to ancient churches to aerobatic flying, there will be something that calls to you as different and fun when you put your radar out.

Reformed workaholic

We spend a great deal of our time at work trying to understand what the boss wants and what our customers and clients demand. The problem with this is that we can spend all our time focused on the perspectives of 'significant others' (especially if we add our partner, friends and family members to the list). We can lose our own view. Indeed, when many of my clients are asked, "What do you want?" they are completely stumped.

This is what had happened to Jane. 'I couldn't formulate desires for my life beyond the narrow trajectory of further promotions, salary raises, bigger projects, clients and responsibilities,' she says.

Over the past five years, she has undertaken a personal journey not only to build her own independent business but also to discover herself. She's found out some things that have surprised her, including the realisation that she doesn't have the go-getting results-driven personality profile she believed she had. 'I prefer to take a more leisurely pace than most organisations allow, in order to get things right.'

In giving herself more time and consideration, Jane's discovered a passion for India and Bollywood films that gives her a perspective into a completely different world.

As a result, she says she appears to have finally kicked her work addiction and is planning a month's travelling in India. 'This is something I never imagined before. I am no longer kidding myself about who I really am, I can recognise the energy and effort it costs me to act "out of character" and no longer feel obliged to live up to other people's expectations of me in my own time.'

As we develop our mental resilience, so we release more energy to engage with the world in new and rewarding ways and love our work. We return to that state of flow where we learn, grow and move calmly through life – until we bump into our emotions, which is the aspect of energy that we'll be exploring next.

CHAPTER 4

EMOTIONAL ENERGY

Listen to the Undercurrents

Working through Conflict

You're Already Perfect

Let Go of Self-imposed Blocks

Are you feeling mad, bad, glad or sad today? Like it or not, your emotions bubble away beneath the surface of your behaviour all the time, affecting the quality of your life, relationships and work. Your emotional energy offers a reason to get up in the morning. Without it, you'd merely function like a robot waiting for someone else to power you up.

Think of emotional energy as the power supply for life. Put a group of people in a room together, whether in an office, working together in an operating theatre or enjoying an event in a massive concert hall like London's 02 Arena, and there's scope for an emotional power surge as all the human responses become attuned to one another.

If you were to stop and check back in your diary for a moment over the last three or four days, what emotions would come to mind? Were you cross with yourself or someone else? Do you feel any sadness or regret for something not done or said? Did you feel joy and excitement in your day or were there moments of worry?

Love, joy, fear, sadness, anger, envy and guilt permeate our everyday lives – this is what it is like to be human. It would be naïve to think that when people arrive at work they leave their emotions at home. It's equally naïve to think that the emotions triggered by events of the day are left behind at the office. Men and women are equally affected.

We experience emotion as feelings in relation to our needs, and these are demonstrated to others through our behaviour. No emotion is intrinsically bad; it's just what you are feeling at the time. However, an emotional response has an impact on others as well as yourself. The bully at work takes her anger or fear out on her victim, just as the soccer hooligan whose team has lost a match picks a fight or throws a brick in temper.

As humans living in society with others, we have fundamental needs:

» to be accepted or liked

» to be useful and needed

» to feel a sense of power and control

Times of change and crisis exacerbate our emotional responses and can lead to extremes of behaviour.

My experience of working on a business merger project comes to mind. On most days I witnessed people experiencing a wide range of emotions. The work we were engaged in often brought out the best in people; but at other times the pressures also brought out the worst.

On a March afternoon, it snowed heavily and I was unlucky to be stuck in an office due to a freak blizzard. All the major roads were blocked. Staff rallied round to ensure their colleagues were safe in exceptionally dangerous travel conditions. The catering manager even walked back to the office through the snow to cook bacon sandwiches for those of us who were stuck.

I was touched by the kindness of several colleagues who I didn't know well, yet who insisted that I didn't attempt to drive in a blizzard. A relative stranger gave me an impromptu picnic made up of all the snacks in his office drawer in case

I got stranded on the motorway. I witnessed people at their kindest and most generous.

At other times, when project teams were working to refine processes and jobs and meet the pressure of deadlines, the work brought out the worst in people. I saw people being insensitive to their colleagues – as fears about job security increased and guilt about the ramifications of the changes began to surface. Senior managers rushed around like whirling dervishes, printing documents and holding conference calls as if their very lives depended on the urgency.

The challenge is whether we befriend the emotions or allow them to taunt and control us. We all carry our emotional history with us, based on memories and experiences that go back through our lives not just to last weekend, but to the time before we worked, into our education years and childhood. As you work through this chapter, consider the emotional highs and lows of your own life and how they impact on your current behaviour.

LISTEN TO THE UNDERCURRENTS

Dan Goleman coined the phrase Emotional Intelligence, known as EQ, which relates to the ability to rein in your emotional impulses, read another's innermost feelings and handle relationships smoothly.

When we are 'emotionally intelligent' we are clear and competent in two areas:

1. Self-awareness – of our feelings and patterns of
    behaviour.

2. Awareness of other people's emotions – and how we relate to them.

EQ enables us to be authentic without getting caught up in our own emotional turmoil, and encourages us to be sensitive to others around us. It is a valuable skill for life.

Whether you are a young intern starting out on your career or a senior professional developing your leadership profile, your ability to work with emotional intelligence can mean the difference between success and failure. It's equally valuable for those whose work is within the home in developing strong relationships with family and friends.

EQ is not something you are born with; you develop it over time, sometimes by investing in your own personal development through courses and coaching – as well as books like this. Healthy EQ makes the difference between you keeping a customer or partner happy or them being totally fed up with you.

Exercise

Leaks and peaks

Certain situations or people can destabilise our emotional wellbeing. Some cause leaks in emotional energy, draining us and taking us low. Other situations raise our adrenalin high, making us feel excited.

Here are some examples of situations that may have an emotional effect. Identify any that you recognise can impact on you as well as noting your own challenges.

	Peaks What needs to happen for me to experience a high burst of energy?	**Leaks** What needs to happen for me to experience a low dip in energy?
Quantity of work		
Quality of work		
Deadlines		
Relationships		
Family responsibilities – for spouse, children, elders		
Health – concerns or habits		
Promotions and appraisals		
Sponsorship by someone/working with others		
Other		

Although we talk about the emotional and physical as if they are separate, they are naturally part of the whole experience of being human. We carry our emotions with us physically and they have a dramatic effect on our wellbeing. In her book *The Molecules of Emotion*, pharmacologist Candace Pert outlines her pioneering research that shows the extent of this body-mind integration in that our emotional memories are stored, mainly through neuropeptides and their receptors, in the cells of our bodies.

As we become aware of what triggers an emotional reaction, we can find ways to defuse that reaction if it is not serving us. For example, Carole was a new teacher who dreaded working with a group of 15-year-olds and became exceptionally angry when they arrived casually dressed in her food technology class. Beneath her anger was the knowledge that she would never have been allowed to dress in such an informal way at her own much stricter school. Her mentor advised her to go to each lesson imagining what the students would all be like at the age of 30 and to remind herself that they would grow up into young people equipped to cook delicious nutritionally balanced meals thanks to Carole's efforts. Lesson by lesson, Carole defused her own emotion, began to appreciate her students' exuberance and listen to their problems. As she became less frustrated with them, they took more interest in her lessons, even entering into Master Chef competitions.

Your body and your emotions

As you tune in to your body you may learn to recognise the link between your physical symptoms and the emotional weight that you are carrying: on the back of your neck, as a pain in your stomach or as a feeling that you could run for miles with joy. Negative emotions are the root cause of unhelpful habits like smoking, bad eating, and alcohol and drug abuse. To change such behaviours we need to become aware of the emotional triggers that compound them.

By focusing greater attention on the emotional triggers for the unwanted behaviour, we can choose the changes that we want to make. While writing this book, I became interested in the effect of emotional states on patterns of eating and drinking. Simply by keeping a note of my emotional mood in a food diary, I recognised certain patterns. For example, on a 'work' day, by late afternoon, I was regularly reaching for a fix of strong coffee and something sweet to go with it. By planning a better quality lunch and a mid-afternoon healthy snack and drink break, I avoided the dip in my blood sugar levels that affected my mood, which in turn meant I dropped excess physical weight.

Weighed down by guilt

Feelings of guilt can sit heavily within us, weighing us down both physically and emotionally. There's plenty of scope for guilt as people question whether they have made the right decisions for themselves, their colleagues, their families and themselves.

Changing pace

As a marketing director with a mobile phone company, Tina built a reputation as someone who always set high standards for herself. She worked hard and delivered projects speedily.

She was head-hunted to take on a high profile directorship with a competitor based on her reputation for turning around difficult situations. Yet, she surprised her colleagues by turning it down.

The remit of the new directorship was demanding and Tina felt she was destined to fail under the pressure. As she contemplated the opportunity, she experienced a real sense of a cold weight on the back of her neck and listened to the message from her body. She realised she no longer had the hunger for the demanding job: 'I wanted to leave at the top of my game, on a high.'

However, she also felt very guilty at turning down an opportunity to earn enough in a year to cover several years of work in a lesser paid job. She felt it was selfish, in some ways, to opt for the easier work option while her husband was still doing a higher paid job.

Yet she really values the opportunity to work at a slower pace. She has a dog that she can walk twice a day and mixes with people in her local village. None of this was previously possible because of the long working hours and commute she had.

It has taken a period of adjustment for Tina to let go of her guilt about her shorter working week and taking a new job that is less intellectually challenging. At first, she was looking over her shoulder to see who would spot her playing truant from work. Now she believes that her husband has gained by having a wife who's bouncing around with energy and their life in the village is richer as a result. 'I had a sense that something was missing, and it's becoming clearer that I had built up a whole persona around my career identity as a company director. That is not who I am.'

Curiosity empowers you

Just as Tina has found it takes time to adjust to a quieter job role, many parents will identify with the opposite impact that comes with a new addition to the family.

When I passed a young friend, Cherie, in town, I realised that she was carrying her beautiful newborn son snuggled inside the baby carrier. As I retraced my steps to offer my congratulations she burst into tears of frustration. 'It's terrible. The birth was so easy in comparison to this lack of sleep.'

I was instantly taken back 20 years to the experience of my own new baby who delighted in screaming her lungs out 24/7 and how I spent hours taking her out for walks or round shops to help me feel that life was sane. Hindsight teaches us the truth: babies with colic grow up. To the impartial outsider, the baby is a dear, innocent creature. To the exhausted mother, the baby is momentarily a demented monster, tormenting her hormones.

For women like Cherie, used to holding down a busy job, motherhood can feel like a huge emotional shock and loss of control as well as having to contend with the major physical changes happening in their bodies. 'I like my life to be organised,' Cherie affirms.

Parenting teaches you, as do many life experiences, that the moment you feel you have control, something changes to make you realise you don't. The lessons offered in hindsight by older parents are: 'Go with it; enjoy it while it lasts. Stop trying to be in control all the time.'

The getting of wisdom

Curiosity invites creativity while control stifles it. Socrates said that 'The beginning of wisdom is the acknowledgment of our own ignorance'. Only when we are able to stay in a place of 'not knowing' do we experience the learning that transforms us.

The unexpected always raises the emotional temperature at work too. People may not get the promotions they expect; a company director may be found to be fraudulent; a colleague resigns unexpectedly or has heart failure in the lift. We don't have control over all the elements in a system, so when we operate with a sense of curiosity, we shift our focus of attention from the emotional tension and stress of the situation to looking for solutions.

Curiosity brings with it a childlike sense of wonder that allows you to extract the fun while breaking up the 'stuckness' of a situation. As I spoke to Cherie about life with her new baby, she realised that she was struggling with a new identity as a mum, responsible for the long-term welfare of her baby. Her predictable life was thrown into uncertainty and chaos, and because the baby cried so much, she felt she was flawed in some way as a mother. She thought she should be experiencing a constant cloud of love and joy and instead felt anger, shame and guilt that life with a baby was feeling tough.

When we link our self-worth with our identity in different roles, and that role is not an easy one, we stop trusting ourselves in other areas of our lives. There needs to be a period of readjustment when we shed one aspect of our lives to take on another new and unfamiliar one. Finding quiet space makes a difference in these transition periods – another reason life is tough for new parents.

Savouring the silence

"In the attitude of silence, the soul finds the path in a clearer light and what is elusive and deceptive resolves itself into crystal clearness."

Gandhi

Our thoughts can run riot in our heads unless we deliberately quieten them down.

'Should I have given that person a job, or made that one redundant?'

'Am I working hard enough compared to the rest of the team?'
'I promised I would do that, and now I can't, but I feel I should.'

'Is it OK to come in 30 minutes late because I wanted to take my daughter to school/my dad to hospital?'

'If I'd done a better proposal, we might have won that contract.'

'Should I just check for messages while I'm on holiday?'

Gandhi recognised the impact of silence to enable people to listen and re-connect, and find the path through however tough the issues they faced. Giving ourselves space to be silent can have a huge impact, not just for us as individuals but for the broader society in which we operate that thrives on a treadmill of speed and instant gratification.

If we all took time to be silent instead of eating on the run or in front of the TV – what difference would that make to us in the West with so many in the grip of obesity? If people took more time to be with one another, listening without judgement, how would that impact relationships for the better in societies rife with conflict?

With practice, it is possible in just ten minutes of silence to drill down to the bones of what's important in your life. Try spending ten minutes in silence at the beginning and end of each day to review your day in work and play and the emotions you have experienced. Then consider the quality of emotional energy you want to bring to your life tomorrow. When we give ourselves time to consider our path every day, we ensure that we are living our own life rather than listening to someone else's wishes and desires for us.

Exercise

Emotional check-in

Begin to be aware of your emotional state or mood and the words you'd use to describe your feelings. If you had a temperature gauge, would you feel hot, warm, normal, cool or cold?

Take some silent time right now to check in with yourself. Sit back in a comfy chair to watch the view.

Notice how you can create some silence inside as you quieten down the thoughts and observe the space around you. Pay attention to the colours you see and the feel of the chair beneath you.

Breathe slowly and get back to the core of your being, the place where there is no noise, where you can feel the silence. Breathe in and out, allowing the sounds to come in and letting them go on your out breath.

You don't need more than a few minutes to stop still. However calm you think you feel, give yourself extra moments of quiet time.

WORKING THROUGH CONFLICT

Things don't always go as we plan or wish. People fall out; travel plans are delayed; the economy takes a down turn; accidents happen. Everyday events, however small or large, can trigger a stress reaction that threatens our dreams.

One of the best pieces of advice in business is 'pick your battles wisely', meaning only fight for the things that are really important and let the rest go unless it's worth the energy. I'm not recommending that you allow people to tread on you or that you act against your principles, simply that you check the emotional cost of a battle in a very practical way. Those who are most flexible usually win in the long term.

By recognising our own emotional reactions and taking responsibility for them it becomes possible to find ways to distance ourselves from everyday fights and problems, and to stop taking everything personally. If you choose your battles wisely and maintain a broader view, you will be able to keep perspective and preserve your emotional energy. Know that what's important is to spread positive energy on our travels so that people feel listened to and respected and more likely to take responsibility for their own reactions.

Off the roller-coaster

The roller-coaster ride at a theme park can be fun in short bursts of scary and exhilarating moments. When you get off you feel giddy and disoriented. Yet that quickly wears off, leaving you with a sense of achievement for facing your fear and arriving safe and unscathed.

In real life, the roller-coaster ride can last a long time, as architect Françoise has found. Recurring bouts of illness, loss of a corporate career and the end of her marriage were low spots in a fast-moving life that centred on adventure holidays, international travel and her work on award-winning buildings.

Her emotions ranged through spells of joy, anger, grief, sadness and fear to lead her to a place where she can let go of much of what has happened with a sense of love and kindness.

*Life changed when she gave up her successful career in a leading archi-
tectural practice to accompany her scientist husband, Manu, on an
assignment to Latin America. One week she was working in Paris,
the next she was an ex-pat wife in Rio de Janeiro.*

*To the outsider, the life of a company wife can look like one enticing
social whirl, yet Françoise soon discovered a huge sense of grief at the
loss of her professional status. 'I no longer felt value for being me. I was
Manu's wife and expected to support him and his company. Work has
a huge social health benefit; it gives me structure, validity, praise and
a sense of achievement. Without work that needed to be done today,
I began to leave everything until tomorrow.'*

*One perk of the job was to head off on a challenging expedition, but
Françoise was unlucky to catch a virus that left her with ME. She went
from being a physically strong woman to lying on the sofa for days on
end. Resentment set in as she found it tough to accept being idle. 'Some
days, all I could do was look at the tree outside the window.'*

*A simple note kept on her bathroom mirror offered valuable emotional
insight at a critical time. It read:*

*'The people who have the best lives are those who make the best
of the lives they have.'*

*Françoise recognised that even on days when she felt physically very
weak, she could strum a few notes on her guitar. From this beginning,
she developed an interest in folk music.*

*The illness also accompanied a breakdown in Françoise's marriage. The
fact that she could no longer share the outdoor life of skiing and moun-
taineering with Manu left them pursuing separate weekend interests,
and Françoise went through further spells of emotional lows: 'I also
grieved my position as a married woman. I didn't want to be single
again and thinking of dating in my late thirties.'*

*Now Françoise has taken a part-time role with a small practice and
paces her energy carefully. Because it's easy for her to over-work, she*

deliberately manages her rest periods. 'I have a 70 per cent rule in my work and social life, which means I rest before I need to. I can't afford to let my batteries run down so low again.

'I think it was Jung who said that the map for the morning of your life may not be the map for the afternoon. I thought I had my life and career mapped out happily. I've had to change the map.'

Today, Françoise says that she has stepped off her roller-coaster exist-ence, smoothed out the highs and lows to navigate a more stable route. She feels that it's better to seek contentment than pursue an exalted sense of happiness.

'I take pleasure in being curious about everyday life instead of seeking only the highs.'

Not getting hooked into the story

It would have been tempting for Françoise to get sucked into playing the victim, dwelling in self-pity. Instead she had the maturity to step back and reflect on her situation. We're not always able to be so detached.

One of the most useful tools I've found in dealing with conflict situations is Steven Karpman's 'Drama Triangle'. Karpman's work builds on the ideas of Eric Berne and his famous Transactional Analysis concepts formulated in the 1950s. Berne talked about the 'games' we play unconsciously that motivate how we interact with people. A 'game' is an unconscious belief that directs our action in a particular way which in turn runs the 'script' that is going on in our heads.

The Drama Triangle describes the dynamics of power, responsibility and vulnerability. Often the game is played out unconsciously between just two people regularly switching

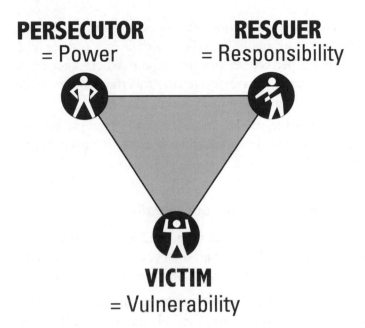

PERSECUTOR
= Power

RESCUER
= Responsibility

VICTIM
= Vulnerability

positions. It also happens with larger numbers of people in family groups, teams and large organisations. The positions are:

Victim – someone who feels vulnerable, powerless and does not take responsibility, where the script is 'Can you help me?' When they can't be rescued any longer and have to be responsible, they switch to persecuting their rescuer.

Rescuer – someone who often seeks to 'rescue' those they see as vulnerable without owning their own vulner-ability, and whose script is 'I'll help you'. They often do more than their share of the work, and switch to Victim or Persecutor mode when they have had enough.

Persecutor – someone who doesn't realise their own power and actually feels like a victim or a rescuer who is being persecuted by others, and where the script comes out as 'You're not getting this right' while inside they are feeling 'I've had enough of this.'

As you can see, all of the roles in the triangle are negative, so the sensible approach is to extract yourself from the drama.

How the drama plays out in daily life

Imagine the marriage between Fred and his wife Frances. They have been playing their own version of the drama game for decades, raising the emotional interest in their lives.

Fred is a self-employed bricklayer and his income has good years and bad years. He feels he does the lion's share of the work (because he only remembers the high earning years) as well as running the home. He sees himself as Frances' rescuer. She has a steady job working for a local authority, but is so tired she can't cook or be sociable in the evenings. 'She's a faddy eater, I have to cook,' he complains.

Frances, meanwhile, feels that she rescues Fred who hasn't the staying power of a 'proper' job that pays the mortgage and pension. She feels that she gets the rough end of the deal some days, yet likes the security of managing all their financial affairs and not sharing that information with him. 'He's clueless about money, so I have to keep him in check,' is the script that she runs.

Over the years, they have regular arguments, each accusing the other of not pulling their weight, but they muddle through with their division of jobs. Until one day Frances discovers that her husband has been having an affair. Whoosh. She escalates into persecutor mode and he retaliates fast. They fly round the other triangular roles of rescuer and victim. She accuses him of being lazy and useless while he pulls out the stops and tells her what a lousy homemaker she is. The hurtful accusations will take them to the divorce court unless they choose a new game to play.

To disentangle themselves from all the emotional energy wasted in the Drama Triangle, Fred and Frances need to do three things:

1. Take responsibility for their actions, and allow others to do the same.
2. Recognise their vulnerability and communicate that honestly.
3. Own their own power to take care of themselves and recognise the impact on others.

When we find ourselves in highly charged conflict situations, it's worth checking which role we might have unconsciously been taking.

» Are we trying to play the hero who knows best and rescue everyone?
» Are we being a victim who doesn't really want to take responsibility for our part in the scenario?

» Or are we starting to be really tough and persecute those around us without recognising the power we have to hurt them?

Exercise

Exiting the drama

Find a time when you have been caught up in a conflict and played the game of rescuer, victim or persecutor as described in the Drama Triangle above - perhaps you were good at all three roles! Ask yourself these questions:

» Who was taking responsibility for whom?

» Where was I vulnerable?

» What got in the way of me owning my power?

» What would I do differently another time?

Embracing the darker emotions

Stephen Cope, a psychotherapist and one of the leading figures at the Kripalu Yoga Centre in Massachusetts, tells the story of an older lady whose husband lives in a nursing home. She is experiencing feelings of dizziness whenever she's about to go and visit her husband. Cope encourages her to sit with and consider the impact of the physical sensation in her body and the feelings that come up. She realises she is feeling on the verge of rage at her husband for abandoning her, a feeling that was unacceptable for her to vocalise. As soon as she allows herself to feel it, her symptoms disappear. Cope argues that until she felt her rage, she couldn't feel her love again.

It's tempting to divide emotions into the good and the bad: the good being the love, joy, happy ones; the bad being the sad and angry. We are either a 'glass half full' person or a 'glass half empty' person.

We would only be partially human if we denied there is a natural place inside each of us for the darker emotions such as sadness, loneliness, cruelty, fear and anger. Often we try to shut these off as unacceptable and, when we do so, we close a door on part of ourselves and our natural energy. We're saying: 'This is how I 'should' feel,' when in fact we feel the opposite.

When we acknowledge the darker emotions we accept what it is to be truly human and authentic and stop suppressing some of the pain of our existence. It can be a very healing place to explore.

In *The Dark Side of the Light Chasers*, Debbie Ford explains how we hide or deny the dark side of our personality. After all, we want (in the main) to be clean-living, decent human beings with all those values of honesty, respect and love for others.

Yet, if we have the capacity to notice the nastier character-istics in others, then there is a part of ourselves (which is generally kept under wraps in decent society) that could also be like that in particular circumstances. You see the bully at work, the controlling power or the greedy person who takes the last slice of the cake. Even the most 'upright citizen' has the potential to commit a crime against another human being.

Ford argues that once we accept our negative qualities then it is possible that these are hidden strengths. The ability to be selfish may be just what we need to prevent ourselves being overwhelmed by others' needs. The ability to get angry means that we have a way to state our views and get our needs met.

In this way, the dark side is as important for us as the light side, in order to be whole people.

> ### Thought provokers
>
> Think about characteristics that you do not like in others. Who really annoys or upsets you? What is it that they do?
>
> Then turn it around: where is the part of you that can also be, for example, unkind, outspoken, spiteful or envious? Make a note of how that can show up in your own behaviour, and explore what the benefits are to you when you behave 'badly'.
>
> Use this information as you wish to enrich your message to yourself. For example, if you are paying attention to getting better at something like martial arts, painting, or customer service, what are the lessons from the dark side?
>
> How can these traits inform your understanding of the human complexity of a colleague, partner or friend?

YOU'RE ALREADY PERFECT

Fear drives a lot of business behaviour, leaving in its wake executives who are stressed and anxious. The fear of not being good enough at work is a common theme amongst even the most outwardly successful and confident people.

William is a bright and energetic man in his early 40s who has enjoyed a highly successful career on the fast track in his professional services firm. Invite him to speak at a conference and he'll happily engage with an audience of 100 people and enjoy every minute of it. See him with his team and he comes across as capable, committed and confident.

William opened a coaching session by saying to me: 'You know, Kate, what this is really about is that I'm fed up with feeling an impostor; that someone's going to find me out.'

As he told me more, he pointed out he had been lucky up until now; his career had gone so smoothly. He'd had a succession of supportive bosses who mentored him. 'I've been in the right place at the right time; that sort of thing.'

William then put his hands on his stomach and explained that he had a real fear inside that, 'I'm going to get rumbled'. People will realise that he didn't know as much as they thought. He believed that he's good at giving the impression that he's more competent than he truly is.

'I really don't think I'm good enough for this next promotion. I don't actually believe in myself. And if I don't believe in me, how can I expect anyone else to?'

As we explored a whole collection of William's beliefs about himself during the session, it became clear that he was habitually discounting clear evidence and facts about his own talents and capabilities, the projects he'd completed against the odds, the strong relationships he'd built. He had stopped acknowledging that he is a successful, competent and smart manager and was experiencing strong self doubt and feelings of being a professional fraud.

How to recognise 'impostor syndrome'

Psychologists have a name for such feelings of inadequacy which takes a huge amount of emotional energy in the workplace and stops people enjoying themselves. They call it the Impostor Syndrome. People with Impostor Syndrome will display certain characteristics. They may, for example:

1. Put their achievements down to luck
2. Ignore their successes
3. Feel like a fake who is going to get found out
4. Over-internalise failure
5. Feel a great pressure not to fail
6. Work extremely hard
7. Convince themselves that they are not intelligent or able

At any one time, most of us can probably identify with some of these characteristics, or know someone who does. They may become significant in certain situations or times in our lives.

In William's case, they came to the fore when he faced a new challenge which required that he step up to take on more responsibility and visibility in his career. Through coaching and personal development we can work with these kinds of impostor feelings and find practical strategies to overcome them.

The impostor syndrome is associated with high achieving, highly successful people, especially gifted men and women like you! It's somewhat different from the idea of low self-esteem because there is a gap between a person's real achievement and a person's perception of the achievement.

Research seems to indicate that certain family backgrounds and dynamics contribute to impostor feelings – where families have unrealistic standards, are very critical or even support a child to the point of believing they are 'perfect' or 'superior', an image that proves too hard to live up to in reality.

Taming the emotional chatter

When writing *Building Self-Confidence for Dummies*, Brinley Platts and I created a whole range of tools to enable you to listen to yourself, affirm your natural talents and find your true inner voice as opposed to the negative chattering gremlins that invade from time to time.

Here are three ways to tame the voice that suggests you're a fraud:

1. Picture a friendly parrot on your shoulder, programmed with a positive message to repeat every time it hears a negative thought: 'I was chosen because I'm the best.' 'I can do this.' 'I am good enough.' 'I'm going to show you just how good I really am.'

2. Imagine the negative voices playing on your CD player, then turning the volume control down to a hushed whisper, and finally gently flicking the off switch. Take the CD out, cut it up, and throw it away.

3. Look for the positive intention of the negative voice. Figure out how it's trying to help you. Acknowledge it, thank it, and tell it to head away now that it's served a useful purpose.

You can clear out those unwanted messages. In their place, decide what is the one message you'd like to hear each day to remind you that you are truly good enough; absolutely perfect just the way you are? Write it down to remind yourself and post it on your bathroom mirror.

LET GO OF SELF-IMPOSED BLOCKS

As human beings we're very clever at tripping ourselves up. We've seen in the earlier chapters how it is more likely to be our own thoughts, our interior world, that ultimately get in the way of us living and working with free-flowing energy, rather than anything that happens in the external world. Did you, for example, look around you and spot what has gone wrong today? Or did you notice what's gone right and let the rest sink into the background?

Albert Einstein is famously quoted (and perhaps misquoted) as saying: 'The most important question to ask: "Is the universe a friendly place?"' Putting this question into the context of personal energy, if you truly believe that the universe is a friendly place, then your energy naturally comes from a good, happy, abundant and positive source.

Just as people can stand in the way, our own beliefs and assumptions can block us. Blocking thoughts such as: 'I have to', 'I should', 'I ought to', will impede your emotional energy. When you find yourself making such statements, check in with yourself to find out what you really want to do. Check whether you are following your own agenda or one that someone around you has come up with. Replace negative thoughts with phrases such as: 'I choose to' and 'I want to', seeing the difference it makes to your energy.

In my 30s, I took on a job as an account director for a PR company which turned out to be a wrong move. There were wonderful perks in terms of smart events, concert and theatre treats and stays at the best hotels in town. Yet I found myself working for a man who lacked decent values; who was dishonest with the clients and his staff.

It took several months for me to understand why I was waking at four in the morning and feeling so anxious about work. At an emotional level, by staying in this work I was buying into the same underhand way of operating which didn't fit with me. I then woke up to the fact that I didn't have to stay. I had the choice to leave a 'good job' that was a poor fit. When I resigned with no other job lined up, the relief was phenomenal. I soon bounced back to my normal optimistic self and attracted new work that was fun and honest. Not once, as I shifted to choose the kinds of colleagues to work with, have I regretted that move, nor at other times subsequently of acting according to my own values and beliefs.

When you hear yourself say that you can't do something, turn the statement on its head to ask: 'And why not?' to get to the heart of what it is that really holds you back. It's a waste of a life to operate according to beliefs that served us well in the past but which are past their sell-by date.

Replacing old beliefs

Richard enrolled on a weekend Pilates' workshop to enable him to understand how the core exercises would improve his golf swing. Yet as the day approached he felt an increasing sense of anxiety in his stomach. When he acknowledged his vulnerability, he said: 'I guess I'm afraid that everyone will know each other, especially all of the women, and I won't be accepted.'

Since the age of five or six, when he found it extremely difficult to be part of the rough-and-tumble boys' gang in the school playground, he feared breaking into any group that already knew each other, especially cliques of women.

His childhood belief that 'groups are not friendly places for me' still drove his behaviour in his 30s. In looking at the one belief, he realised there were others too, about how women were unfriendly.

Working on his own development, he came to recognise that he is a strong and humorous man. He reworded his apprehension about joining new groups to become: 'I've chosen to be there and learn together', safe in the knowledge that he already has the means to charm people and be accepted.

Earlier in this chapter we looked at the question of guilt, an emotion that can really block people from attempting to do what they really want to do. People who are used to being busy can get into the habit of creating extraordinarily demanding lists of things they have to do, even at weekends. Many of my 'successful' clients clear lists of tasks only to create a new, longer list. They feel guilty about being idle. If this sounds familiar, then it can be worth checking out what beliefs you have around relaxation and leisure time – the things you 'should' and 'ought' to be doing.

A final word about money

One subject guaranteed to make people feel all those emotional highs and lows of mad, bad, glad and sad is money. On the plus side, money can buy opportunities and freedom. On the down side, money can inspire greed and envy. In the words of the old Beatles song: 'Money can't buy you love'. And love is the most healing and powerful emotion that we all need.

Money is a huge personal driver, with the ability to furtively turn up the emotional temperature everywhere you go. Attitudes and beliefs around wealth build through generations, organisations and cultures until we lose sight of the fact that money is a means to an end, not an end in itself. Whole books and seminars are devoted to the energy of money and so, before concluding this chapter, spend some time exploring your own beliefs around money to clean up any emotional energy loss.

Exercise

Your emotional relationship with money

Take a piece of paper and make a note of your responses to the following:

What does having money do for you? What benefits does it give you in terms of, for example, peace of mind or security, power, freedom, choices or control?

How does money affect how you feel? If you acted as if you had a million pounds in the bank, how would that affect the work you do? If you had nothing in the bank, how would that affect the work you do?

What about your self-worth? How is that affected by the money you have or earn?

Notice the effect that your money has on your emotional energy and if you might need to change anything in how you think or behave in order to allow your energy to flow freely.

When we develop a confident and healthy relationship with money, and understand our true worth, then we resist the temptation to live out our lives driven by money and other people's expectations about it. We then find it's a resource that flows in and out. Sometimes there's plenty and at other times it's in short supply.

Money is simply one currency. Of course, you need enough to live on, but that's all you need, and when we stockpile it, living in a state of fear of not having enough, that can lead to a paralysis of choices in the here and now.

Ostensibly we all work for the money; yet that's only part of the juicy emotional cocktail that bubbles below the surface as we come to work. The real joy we feel at work comes in subtle ways with characteristics such as increased status, learning, power, freedom and connections with others all playing their part in making us feel emotionally satisfied and increasing the state of flow that we talked about in Chapter 3.

Ultimately, we need a sense of passion and purpose, to feel valued and worthwhile. When we can find this deeper emotional connection to our work, we gain a sense of delight that money alone will not give us; more on this in Chapter 5 when we move into the realms of values and contribution to a larger world.

PURPOSEFUL ENERGY

Access your Passion

Abundance Wins over Control

Breathing in the Power

Gather Energy from the Natural World

Develop Deeper Connections

I n this chapter we're looking at purposeful energy. This is
the kind of energy that comes from spending our time
in meaningful ways, with a sense that it's well directed and
has a positive impact for others beyond the material reward
or personal recognition. You might also call this a kind of
spiritual energy, not because of any religious connotations,
but because it feeds our spirit and brings us alive.

Ask any group of people what 'work' means to them and
you get as many individual definitions as people in the
group. When I asked several business owners for their
thoughts, one answered: 'Work would be something that
I do in return for money where I don't have any choice
because I have to earn the money and be in a certain
place at a certain time. This is "work" but it's not WORK,
because I'm doing something I love doing.' Another said: 'I
love what I do because of who I am. Work keeps me alive,
yet I still call it work.' They came to an agreement: 'I guess
what we're talking about here is work as a vocation, a calling. We feel privileged to do this work and feel passionate
about it.'

Doing work that feels superficial and is undervalued reduces
self-esteem and leads us to feel 'small' within ourselves. For
many, the love of work is related to the knowledge that
we're making a difference to someone, somewhere; that we
are part of something worthwhile or successful; the belief
that what we do is important and has a purpose.

In the parlance of Joseph Campbell's hero's journey,
mentioned in Chapter 1, we have heard the 'call to adventure' and 'stepped over the threshold'. Meaningful work has
personal value beyond the daily tasks we do, and when we

can't identify that meaning or hold onto it, we sense that we need either to rediscover the connection or choose to do something different.

For many years in my early career I created corporate literature: business magazines, brochures and newsletters which were written, designed and printed to a deadline – work that I loved. Most of the work was interesting and valuable; I thrived on meeting new people, hearing their stories and communicating information so that complex ideas and products could be understood by all. Those hours of listening, sifting and reshaping words set the foundation for my later work as a coach.

Every job has its frustrating times and one incident stands out as a trigger for change. I was producing a magazine for a client on a ridiculously tight schedule, against the odds. I pushed, pummelled and pulled in favours to meet the deadline. Suppliers were working overnight and at weekends to get the job delivered on time. Several days after the stunning publications were printed, I had not heard a murmur from the client, which was surprising considering the wave of activity that had gone before.

Feeling concerned that it hadn't been well received, I telephoned: 'Just calling to see what you thought of the magazine.' I sensed the embarrassment in the tentative response of the marketing director who acknowledged that he hadn't actually seen the finished magazine. He made a couple of internal telephone calls while I hung on the line, finally saying 'Oh, it's fine. They're all sitting in Goods Inward.' The call ended curtly with no thanks just a 'Talk soon, I've a meeting to get to.'

Frustration, anger and disillusionment kicked in as I realised I'd been given an artificially tight deadline, putting many people under pressure unnecessarily. It seemed that the client hadn't cared about the work as much as we had. My sense of purpose had been deflated; the value of what I was doing was diluted. As this connected with a few other similar experiences, I began to hear the call to a new adventure and recognised that I was ready to shift my career focus. My purposeful energy needed to be focused in a direction that renewed my sense of self.

Whether you are a pensions clerk, insurance salesman, dentist, oil rig engineer or the owner of a bed and breakfast business, you need to stay connected to your sense of purpose and to know that the burden of the work you do is an acceptable load to carry. We can earn a living in all kinds of ways, but there's nothing more soul destroying than putting in the hours without a sense that it's meaningful.

You may never know the impact you've had on those you connect with at the time you do your work. In order to increase your sense that your work is worthwhile, spend a while considering the possible benefits to others in the longer term, by asking 'What does my work do for others?' For example, on the face of it, selling insurance or writing computer software seems a soulless transaction until you realise the security or assistance it provides to those on the receiving end of your product or service.

John was an English teacher at a boys' school for more than 20 years, and the imposition of government inspections and more paperwork took its toll on his health. He left conventional teaching to set up a tennis academy and returned to schools to run tennis sessions that he loved, with pupils who wanted to be there and have fun.

Some years later, one of John's ex-pupils became a well-known business entrepreneur and invited John to take part in a television documentary as one of the most important influences on his teenage years. Suddenly, all those years of teaching and the hard slog involved were validated because someone showed their appreciation for John's integrity and efforts. He felt proud of his work once more because he had been recognised.

Our emotional attachment to work goes deeper than we realise. When I worked for the computer and electronics giant Hewlett-Packard, I loved being associated with high-quality products known for innovation, reliability and quality. What a tremendous buzz I got from going out to customer sites and seeing the machines in action; whether at a steel stockholder's, cosmetics manufacturing plant, football club or city trading room. At critical moments in my life, I've been reassured by the sight of that familiar HP company logo. When I was giving birth to my daughters, I was linked up to an HP fetal monitor in the maternity unit; and when my father died, I felt a sense that all was OK with the world because the registrar had an HP computer and printer.

The search for meaning

Viktor Frankl's experience of making connections and finding meaning through work are set out in his famous book, *Man's Search for Meaning*. At the heart of his therapeutic work is the belief that, whatever circumstances we find ourselves in, what keeps us going through the ups and downs is the ability to find meaning in our lives. We need to locate that connection to stay content even in the darkest times, as Frankl's own life demonstrated, having survived captivity in Nazi death camps, including Auschwitz.

When one of Frankl's patients suffered a crisis in their lives, he would seek to enable them to reconnect with their purpose in three different ways:

1. Making them **appreciate the fuller value** of everything they had achieved, created or accomplished – yet often dismissed. As, for example, the teacher who guided thousands of pupils in their learning and set an enthusiastic role model for them even though he was frustrated by bureaucracy.

2. Encouraging them to relive a powerful experience – whether capturing the view from a mountain top, a great performance or love for another person. These 'peak experiences' remind people of life's wonders even when suffering a low spot.

3. Finding the powerful and positive meaning by reframing apparently dire situations. For example, take the insurance salesman who hands over the 'death in service' benefit cheque to a widow; through his work, he provides a secure future for her and her young family.

ACCESS YOUR PASSION

When we find the passion, that deep enthusiasm in our lives, it creates an energy force all of its own. The poet, David Whyte, recalls talking about his work-related exhaustion with his friend, a wise monk. The monk told him: 'The antidote to exhaustion is not sleep. The cure is wholeheartedness.'

When you are committed to what you are doing, your energy can feel boundless. Your passion captures your whole heart. Use your purposeful energy to begin to notice the peaks and troughs in everyday life: those times when you've connected with extremes of emotion. The aim is then to let go of half-hearted activity or to transform it into wholehearted activity.

Some people almost attack work with a passion from an early age. They have a strong sense of calling and vocation. Luisa knew from her teenage years growing up in war-torn Europe that she wanted to be a medic who made a massive difference in the world. Her medical training in Rome set her on a path to become the first doctor in a small mountain village in Italy and then to study tropical medicine and head off to remote parts of Africa. She has a strong sense of her identity as a doctor, willing to tackle any challenge, who recognises that her sense of calling continues to give her days meaning. Although now retired, she volunteers her services in a small hospital, translates medical papers for colleagues and treats patients who have no means to pay.

For others, passion develops in a steadier way; there may not be a particular named profession or role that provides a single clear direction; the path we have trodden becomes visible only with hindsight. Frank has undertaken many different jobs, constantly refining the work that he does, from hairdresser to restaurant manager to Shiatsu teacher. He is willing to grow and learn, following his current interests.

The common thread he detects is his talent for calm service: making clients feel good, relaxed and nourished.

You can tune into your passion as you pay close attention to activities that ignite your energy.

Exercise

Finding your passion – the DASE model

Learn from the peaks or troughs of your experience. Your energy is fired up by the extremes of what pleases you and what makes you mad.

Best of times	Delighted	Ecstatic
Worst of times	Angry	Sad

Identify the best and worst of times:

D – when have you been **delighted,** experiencing a gentle sense of joy and feeling blessed with life?

A – when have you been **angry,** disgusted, experiencing the trough of despair?

S – when have you been **sad,** disappointed and low?

E – when have you been **ecstatic,** experiencing the peak of exuberance and wellbeing?

As you consider the best and worst of times, what ideas emerge about your sense of purpose? Begin by noticing what you do when you stand up for what you care about, which in turn makes a difference to others.

Create a statement of purpose. Capture your thoughts in a simple and positive sentence that begins: I am someone who... and include in your sentence a connection with people, places and situations that extend beyond yourself and the here and now.

Here are examples:

I am someone who...

> creates harmony and understanding in schools
>
> provides healing for those with no money
>
> makes mobile phone services easy for non-technical people to understand
>
> creates a welcoming home for family and guests
>
> encourages older people to remain active
>
> helps clients secure their finances safely for all stages of their lives
>
> fosters safe waste disposal to protect the environment for future generations
>
> makes the office a better place to work through my sunny smile

It is possible to create your own sense of meaning in any purposeful activity, from washing dishes and sweeping the streets through mundane administrative tasks, to high profile activities such as an award winning architect or President of the United States.

As you work with this sense of meaning and awareness of your personal contribution, you operate from a feeling of self-confidence and on a safe footing. The challenge is then to break out of playing small and staying safe by stretching yourself and realising your potential. Purposeful energy is sparked as you continue to grow as an individual and eventually it takes on a motivational power of its own.

Starting with values

Recognising your values, the things that drive you and make you tick, provides a strong foundation for living a life that is purposeful and meaningful and which ultimately will give you permission to be yourself. While few people could easily state their life's purpose, with a little work, most can recognise their values and know what is important to them.

Often we learn most about values when they are stamped on or stamped out of us. Dominic is a government official with a strong sense of decency and service to his country. Since studying Economics and Languages, he's enjoyed a steady career with several foreign postings. Without exception, he's worked for people who've been straightforward leaders, wanting to get the best out of their staff, who trust bright people to take a project and run with it.

When he finds himself with a new boss, Andrea, who micro-manages and changes her mind frequently, he becomes very stressed. Worst of all, his boss is playing silly political games, doing things that she believes will make her look good in front of the more senior people in the organisation. She changes her mind frequently and insists on taking back control of budgets, meetings and decisions that Dominic is more than capable of making alone. The discomfort of this situation has left Dominic unable to sleep at night and miserable about being at work. 'Suddenly my job has turned into the job from hell.'

Dominic's values have been violated and he has started to question his ability to stay with the organisation he loves. Respect for others and for self is a core value that drives our sense of purpose at work.

Exercise

Values identification

Values lie at the heart of motivation and wellbeing. Knowing what you value in life is probably the most fundamental question you can ask yourself. Begin by asking, 'What is most important to me in my life?' and continue to ask until you have identified a bedrock of core values: a list of 10 or 15 things that are really key for you.

In *Building Self-Confidence for Dummies*, co-authored with Brinley Platts, we devote a whole chapter to uncovering personal values. We distinguish between means values and end values. Means values are a means to an end, while the end values are the real core values.

Once you identify your own list of values, the next question to ask yourself is: 'If I have (value x) what will that give me?' So, for example, money is a means value not an end in itself. For some, money buys freedom, for others it brings power, respect or security.

Here is the initial list of means values for Dominic, who we talked about above:

A well paid job

A boss who leaves me alone

A strong family life

International travel

Time to exercise

Open communication

A mix of friends from different walks of life

Training

A comfortable home where I can relax

Going scuba diving each year

As he takes each means value in turn and asks 'What does this give me?', he sifts the list to come up with his end values which looks like this:

respect

honesty

freedom

security

health

It is not surprising that, when Dominic first encounters a new boss that he does not respect, he finds himself in something of a fix because there is a conflict between his desire for respect and his desire for security. If he resigns from his job he loses his security and he will need to find an alternative way to get that value met. In order to redress the situation he places his values in an hierarchy, scoring them from the most important to the least important. Dominic decides that respect wins over security, and begins to work with his coach to look for a new role or to find a way of working that enables him to hold onto his personal respect even if it's difficult.

Our values exist even if we've never thought about them or articulated them. Being consciously aware of your values and how you need to honour them can make it easier to make decisions and choices in daily life.

Seeking personal mastery

When you live your life according to your values and build purposeful energy, you can shift to a position where you are committed to personal mastery. You can become the hero in your life, stepping up to bigger challenges and reaching your potential rather than passively observing what life brings.

As the Vice-President of Employee Health for a global organisation, Adrian is passionate about unleashing people's full potential. One aspect of his work is to deliver a leading-edge training programme to increase personal resilience and develop levels of engagement and wellbeing. This involves showing people how to get in touch with their passion, define their purpose in life and develop new working habits that honour their core values.

His course demonstrates that applying only a small degree of extra effort can shift us from being 'ordinary' to 'extra-ordinary' in different areas of our lives. 'We encourage people to write a "big story" of how they want their lives to be – their whole lives, not just the work,' he says.

The wellbeing programme includes an exercise about walking an imaginary and dangerous plank. People are invited to say what they would be willing to risk their lives for. Would they put themselves in danger if offered a million pounds, for example? The answer is invariably 'no' even if the stakes are raised to provide increasing levels of wealth. 'Family' is usually the top choice for the people who've been through the training. Yet family gets forgotten and pushed down the list of priorities in the scrabble of a working week. Generating income is seen as more important on a daily basis. However, when our values are compromised and our values are forgotten over time, our purposeful energy is gradually sapped.

As the training programme has been delivered to colleagues around the world Adrian has become increasingly energised by the purpose of his work and it has led him to take on new physical and intellectual challenges in all areas of his life, including martial arts.

What is your legacy?

There comes a time when every new role, project or activity is complete and it is time for you move on. When you finish you will have made your mark, and you leave behind a legacy.

Adrian found that tapping into his spirit through his work released oodles of energy and is now writing a book as his legacy to his family about what he has learnt about personal mastery. The discipline of telling his story of what he is learning as he travels actually changes the way he behaves; 'Writing as I go, and taking my family on my own hero's journey with me, means that I do what I say I'm going to do. It's my commitment to taking action and reminding myself that I'm making the extra effort it takes to shift from ordinary to extraordinary.'

Whatever happens in the minutiae of our lives, we will leave a legacy that gives others a message about the essence of our purposeful energy, the things we cared about and how that shaped our unique contribution to the world. In the following exercise, I invite you to explore what you would like yours to be.

Exercise

Personal legacy story

» Choose a situation that fires you up with a sense of passion, where you recognise the purposeful energy of being delighted, angry, sad or ecstatic (see the DASE model earlier). Find something you care about – at work or at home – and write the story of your legacy. It may relate to a period of time or a particular event such as the birth of your child, the completion of a day's work or even your funeral.

» Think about what others would say about you if they were writing about how they see you in this situation. Would they say that you had been decent, honourable, or stubborn beyond belief? That you had strong values and respect for others, that you had a talent in a particular area such as baking apple cake or coaching the junior football team, a passion for red cars and quirky socks? That you stood up for what you believed in or did everything you could to bend over backwards and please others?

» Take a piece of paper, choose a scenario which has some importance for you and write from the voice and perspective of a colleague or close friend or member of your family. Allow yourself to write for about 10 minutes from the position of observing your life, until you have filled a couple of pages with a flow of thoughts. There is no need to edit it.

» Now take a break, put your words to one side and wander off for a stretch.

» Step back to being yourself once more and read your legacy. Is it one that makes you proud or disappointed in yourself? Are you living your passion or hiding behind others? Ask yourself: 'Is this a job, a life that you really want to own?'

» Now rewrite your legacy story as you'd truly like it to be. Notice what you change, tweak, remove and edit as you choose to be remembered at your lightest, brightest most extraordinary.

» With your legacy story in place, the next step is to decide on a course of action. What steps do you need to take to live your life to the full and love your work so that you are proud of your legacy? And which one step will you take today?

ABUNDANCE WINS OVER CONTROL

Living in the Western world, the majority of people are unlikely to ever know true hunger and what it is to have to scrape together every scrap of food, hunting through the rubbish bins to feed your family. In tough economic times, it's tempting to become more focused on personal needs than on other people or communities. Yet this is also an opportunity to follow your passion and sense of purpose while forging new connections.

Those who shift their work to embrace a sense of generosity to others and overcome a 'scarcity mentality' will find doors opening to them, a renewed quality of energy and sense of peace with themselves as Viv's story illustrates.

Place to be me

A hobby or other interest may often inspire a longer-term career change, but when Viv took on a voluntary role on the board of a charitable trust, she hadn't anticipated becoming its Chief Executive.

Viv funds her own training and travel and has made several personal donations to the charity to assist its work. Other riches, however, abound every day, when she walks the trust's one-acre site where people come to recover from mental or physical health difficulties and she can see the immediate impact of the trust's work.

'I've found a place where I can be me instead of being a piece of clockwork.'

After 30 years developing her clinical expertise in the NHS, Viv was increasingly feeling 'muffled, buried, and de-personalised'. She gave up the possibility of an early retirement option to move to the charity sector, realising that 'I couldn't spend another seven years of my working life treading water.'

As the Chief Executive, Viv knows that her role is the most visible, yet she has found a freedom at work that was lacking in her previous organisation. 'I don't feel the need to fit in as much, I'm learning loads and I know if ever I become a millionaire, I'll be a philanthropist!'

Soulful business

Viv defines the quality of 'spirituality' in her work. 'I've landed in a place that believes in and truly values wider connections – with nature and the broader community. Yes, it takes energy to work out how I'm going to solve real problems, but this is a soulful business.'

As a qualified clinical psychologist and therapist, Viv has more stamina than most when dealing with emotional 'stuff', and recognises the level of self-care that's needed to protect those working in the charity sector. 'People can get tired when dealing with needy clients and now I can use my clinical and coaching skills to help staff develop healthy ways of working.' She uses her own 'Mindfulness' practice to pay attention to what is going on in her mind and body on a day-to-day basis. 'This has been very helpful in staying calm and accepting whatever happens as the place where we are at.'

She inherited an organisation with an outdated vision, reduced income and a defunct business plan, plus several people who didn't live up to the espoused values. With a challenging job on her hands to turn the charity around, she's fully aware of keeping this work sustainable for herself as well as the community.

She believes in explaining the 'why' behind change, as well as the 'what', helping individuals to make sense of why things may need to be different. 'It generally leads to a smoother change process in my experience, yet so many leaders leave the 'why' bit out and wonder why staff resist. It's about treating your staff and colleagues as adults.'

BREATHING IN THE POWER

Breathing allows energy to flow through us freely – we are literally breathing in the atoms and molecules of the universe as we take in fresh air through our noses. Many life-enhancing practices, such as yoga, meditation and dance, emphasise the power of good breathing practices and the effect on the body and mind. Deep breathing is a simple way to clear the mind and has the power to help us to focus and align us to our purpose. John Grinder, the co-creator of a body of knowledge called Neuro-linguistic Programming (NLP), explains that breathing changes how your body feels and reacts, which changes your emotional state which then affects your performance in any activity.

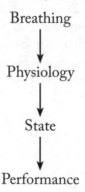

The genius of breathing, compared to other involuntary bodily functions such as blood pumping from the heart, is that it happens unconsciously while we sleep, yet we can consciously change the way we breathe. In a relaxed state, breathing naturally slows down; in a highly alert state, breathing naturally quickens. As we deliberately change the speed or the movement of breath through the body, we feel the effect on mind as well as body. Learning breath control allows us to remain alert yet calm under pressure.

For thousands of years ancient traditions have made the link between breathing and the state of our minds and bodies; in the yogic texts, and practices from India, China and Tibet. Those who practise arts such as mindfulness, meditation, yoga and tai chi are not only rewarded with better physical health, but they also stay calm and centred; they create an experience with each new breath that enables them to 'stay present' in the moment.

Most people don't know how to consciously breathe freely, and when they take a deep breath they tense the body unnecessarily, contracting the abdomen and straining the upper chest. Just look at how a contented baby breathes easily: its belly and diaphragm expand as it breathes in, contracting back towards the spine as it breathes out. Allow yourself to take a breath like this, and stay relaxed and open.

Learning to breathe is not like learning to paint or play music where you need to learn a new skill. It's about accessing what you already know through every cell of your body; it's the fundamental experience of being alive.

Exercise

Use this classic yoga breathing exercise at any time when you feel under stress and need to get grounded once more.

Hold the fingers of the right hand in front of the face. Rest the index and middle fingers gently on the eyebrow centre. The thumb is above the right nostril and the ring finger above the left. These two fingers will control the flow of breath in the nostrils by alternately pressing on one nostril, blocking the flow of breath, and then the other.

Sit comfortably. Keep the head and spine upright, opening the chest.

1. Close the right nostril with the thumb and breathe in through the left to a count of 1, 2, 3.
2. Close the left nostril with the ring finger, release the pressure of the thumb on the right nostril, and breathe out through the right, to a count of 1, 2, 3.
3. Inhale through the right nostril, 1, 2, 3.
4. Close the right nostril, open the left nostril, exhale through the left nostril 1, 2, 3.

That is one complete round. Practise 10 rounds. When you're comfortable with practising this, gradually increase the count, and make the exhalation twice as long as the inhalation, up to 12:24. This ratio establishes a calming rhythm for your brain and heart, keeping your purposeful energy on track.

Developing self-protection

Following your passion comes with a health warning. Those who are passionate about what they do can be prone to becoming overwhelmed by their work, particularly if they are naturally compassionate and generous to others. Those in the caring professions and charity sector will recognise the theme of 'compassion overload'. Passion for what you do can make you blind to your own wellbeing – physically, emotionally, mentally and socially.

Diana's first husband became so wrapped up in his charity work at weekends with a homeless hostel that she divorced him. With two small children at home and a full-time job, she found his involvement with the charity dominated their family life, leaving no space for a loving relationship. 'He spent less time with the children than the people he was helping, and couldn't even wait to have dinner with us on Sunday,' she says. 'He was so consumed by the charity that in the end I asked him to move out.'

There is some wisdom in the old phrase that 'charity begins at home.' In the business world, the stretch is always going to be for higher performance and a stronger contribution to the business which can takes its toll on the time we spend with loved ones.

On a flight back into Heathrow one evening, the plane circled the airport for half an hour waiting for a landing slot. As I chatted to my fellow passenger about the delays in air travel, we began to discuss how many hours we spent from home. An elegant lady of around 60 years of age, she smiled and said that she chose to do a job that only required her to travel once in six weeks. Twisting her wedding ring between the thumb and forefinger of her right hand she added: 'At my age, dear, it's much easier to find a new job than a new husband.'

When you are passionate about what you do, your life may be getting more and more frenetic as you aim to cram in more activity. The creative space you need gets lost; your work subsumes your identity and you miss the vital ingredient: self love.

Nourish yourself as well as others. It may sound selfish, and in the true sense of the word it is, because it's about looking out for yourself. You are the person who controls the thermostat of your life, who knows when the temperature is getting too hot, and holds the power to cool things down when necessary. Unless you take control of your personal life as well as your work, then your passion can burn you out. Self love ensures that you live your daily life in a way that is sustainable. Think of self love as an essential layer of protection around your work space.

Top tip

Creating good quality 'down-time' allows you to keep your spirit charged:

1. Develop your home environment to be especially pleasing to return to. Create the space that you love to be in, where you can relax without any jobs to do, just sitting back and enjoying the view, reading a book or playing your favourite music.

2. Feel the breeze on your cheeks and in your hair. Build in times to stretch and breathe outdoors during your day.

3. Move in circles of people who want nothing from you other than your need to nourish yourself. Choose people who energise and lift your spirits so you come away refreshed.

GATHER ENERGY FROM THE NATURAL WORLD

"No longer conscious of my movement, I discovered a new unity with nature. I had found a new source of power and beauty, a source I never dreamt existed."

Roger Bannister, athlete, on breaking the four-minute mile

Regular breaks from the great indoors sustain our spirit and give us a sense of perspective. There are times when we all need to walk around a lake, in the park, the woods, on the beach or up a mountain. Connecting to these positive sources feeds the positive quality of our thoughts and actions, recognising our unity and connection with others. Then we become powerful vehicles to harness this natural energy and make a positive difference in whatever we choose to do.

On sunny mornings when I enjoy the luxury of sitting and writing in my back garden, the energy emanating from the sky is tangible. I listen to the murmur of the grasses in the breeze and the small birds dipping in and out of the water fountain. On cooler days, I find a quiet satisfaction in walking in the mist under a grey sky with the view through the woods clouding into the distance and knowing that the impending rain will come. When I drive along a motorway at the end of a working day, I take in that magically vast expanse of evening sky.

These are the kind of experiences that we can all gather in small and gentle ways every day, to stay connected with the world before we feel depleted. Sunshine and clouds are free to all. The sky stretches out across the horizon, and nature pours forth energy. The trees abundantly produce seed even when left to their own devices and remind us that we don't have to push so hard to get more or do more. Take the opportunity to be in the moment by accepting the gift of your view, wherever you are.

Spouse at home

A change in our work circumstances inevitably has an impact on those we live with. Whether the event is retirement, redundancy or a planned move, there will be a period of adjustment.

When Sarah's husband lost his job, it impacted her work as an artist. She feels a strong need for space without distraction that was lost when he was at home all day. 'Suddenly Brian was moping around and interrupting my work because he had no company and didn't know how to fill his time. His negative energy began to infect me.'

Sarah took herself out to the river for more and more walks alone in order to capture the space she needed for herself. After an hour outside she was able to return with her creative energy revitalised. 'I felt so claustrophobic at home when there were boundaries around my thinking space.'

The upside of this was the development of her work, creating a collection of paintings and photographs inspired by the changing seasons along the waterway. In this way she refocused her purposeful energy.

She says: 'It was also important that Brian was busy and felt needed after losing his job, so I was able to use his IT skills and spare time to help me learn more about digital printing. So it actually enriched the quality of my art in ways that wouldn't have happened if he was still commuting to the city.'

As Sarah was able to relax more into the change, she invited Brian to join her on her walks so he, too, appreciated the ability to take good quality exercise each morning instead of rushing for the early train. Once Brian took a new job, she found that she missed his company; the house was too quiet and she shifted her work to be within a studio of artists.

DEVELOP DEEPER CONNECTIONS

Great leaders like Mahatma Gandhi were not born as international orators with hundreds of thousands of people following them, yet, once driven by their passion, they attract others to them. Gandhi was naturally shy and softly spoken. As a young lawyer travelling in South Africa, he witnessed the injustice of racial discrimination first hand. Gandhi 'heard the call' which fired up his passion for human rights. The cause that he believed in was the pursuit of freedom which led ultimately to his assassination in 1948 after an extraordinary life. His ideas became revered and the person with it; he was living an authentic life with a connection to the world that extended beyond any sense of self.

As we listen to our spirit, our soul, we lose the inhibitions of self-consciousness; our words and actions are not just about us any longer, we are working with something bigger: the values we live and contribution that we make. On his death, Albert Einstein commented that Gandhi was the only statesman to stand for higher human relationships in the political sphere.

A colleague, Tim, who is naturally reserved and shy, has begun addressing large audiences of people for an association that he's part of and feels passionate about. 'It's as if I leave myself on the chair, when I get up to speak,' he says.

'This is about them and not about me.' All kinds of new connections with people have been formed through his work, much of which is done on a voluntary basis, leading to invitations to speak in different countries and meet many wonderful people. 'When we dare to listen to our spirit, all kinds of possibilities open up,' he says echoing the message of Patanjali:

> "When you are inspired by some great purpose, some extraordinary project, all your thoughts break their bounds: your mind transcends limitations, your consciousness expands in every direction and you find yourself in a new, great and wonderful world. Dormant forces, faculties and talents become alive, and you discover yourself to be a greater person by far than you ever dreamed yourself to be."
>
> *Patanjali*, early yoga master and author of the Yoga Sutras, written between 500 and 200 BC

Shift from success to significance

Dewitt Jones is one of America's top professional photographers and a motion picture director who had two films nominated for Academy Awards before he was 30.

Twenty years as a freelance photographer for National Geographic *earned him a reputation as a world-class photojournalist.*

Using his own exceptional photographs as examples, Dewitt now helps people see the world with new eyes and rediscover their own creative gifts. In telling the story of transforming his own work, he shares tales about his work as a photographer who found the extraordinary in an ordinary view by looking at the world through a different lens.

He talks about making a shift from success to significance: 'As I celebrated what was right in the world, I began to build a vision of possibility, not scarcity. By celebrating what is right, we fix what is wrong. We go from being the best in the world to being the best for the world.'

As we develop deeper connections with others, we need to let go of the familiar lens in our own eyes, challenge our beliefs, assumptions, and conventional ways of thinking and working. Just as the photographer gets the stunning shot by coming at a familiar landscape from an unconventional viewpoint, so we gain by turning our conventional thinking on its head.

One way to do this is to extend our networks of connections into new and different fields where we experience the world as others see it. By breaking down barriers in this way between ourselves and others, we connect into the unifying quality of purposeful energy.

Thought provoker

» Where in your life do you sense you could make a bigger contribution for the world?

» What could you shift to the extra-ordinary from what is currently ordinary?

» Take a walk out in nature or shift your view to encompass a natural place where you can ponder the questions.

Coming from an authentic place

Our family backgrounds shape the values we bring into the workplace and then our work in turn shapes the development of the values we take home. To understand what drives a person to become passionate, to contribute and harness their purposeful energy, pay attention to their early influences.

Bryn's story begins with tales of his grandfathers. One, a miner, suffered an accident at the pit where he worked. He was trapped beneath the ground of a collapsed section of the mine for three days; later his job changed and he was put in charge of the bike sheds, which had the benefit of enabling him to connect with everyone at work. The other grandfather was a political activist with five children to feed who struggled to provide a regular income or roof over their heads. His most secure job was as a canal lock-keeper, where the work also provided a tied cottage for the family.

Recognising his legacy of social awareness combined with hardship and poverty, Bryn decided at a young age to be rich.

Grammar school education set Bryn on a path to achieve a standard of living undreamt of by his grandfathers. After university, he took the hippy trail to India and the Middle East, first learning and then teaching meditation with the Maharishi Mahesh Yogi before returning to England to enter the 'real' world of work.

He arrived back in 1970s London to enter the world of computer programming with what he describes as 'mixed-up' attitudes. For the last 30 years he's earned his living amongst the Chief Information Officers and the IT teams of the FTSE-100 companies that he now coaches to become authentic and respected leaders.

Once asked by a London taxi driver, 'What do you do?' he replied with a clear sense of purpose. 'I'm turning large organisations into fit places for decent people to work.'

If we were to map various moves of his working life, it may appear as if he began with a definite career plan and mission, yet the connections on the route only became visible as he travelled it. Certain moves looked risky at the time; often he's left comfortable, secure, well-paid jobs to follow alternative directions that felt more interesting and challenging, investing heavily in his own personal development and sharing ideas along the way.

'When I'm coming from an authentic life-supporting place, it's like a dream, projects become so absorbing that I don't want to do anything else.'

Bryn never planned to become a traditional miner like his grandfather, yet he still digs deep, seeking to make a valuable contribution through his labour. Nor has he become embroiled in a political life; instead the activist roots have fostered his ability to campaign against the 'status quo' of accepting mindless activity as a way of working.

His definition of rich today reaches beyond material wealth. He says: 'Being able to play in an area you want to play; being healthy; raising a family with great values; being an ethical person who really cares about people. That's being rich.

'If you are going to be switched on you need to know your own value, choose how you want your life to be, make a contribution, and choose projects that are bigger than you.'

Notice the difference you create

As you practise approaching every situation and person from a position of purposeful energy, you cannot help but create an impact on those around you. There will be a ripple effect. Give yourself times when you simply appreciate who you are and your contribution to others.

Exercise

Appreciative visualisation

Find yourself a quiet space where you can give yourself a moment to breathe quietly and relax to take in the following words. I recommend that you record them in a slow, gentle voice and play them back to yourself, or invite a friend to read them to you. Allow ample time between sentences to pause and reflect quietly.

Get into a comfortable seated position, close your eyes and focus on your breath. Breathe in and out effortlessly and quietly. Leave the noise around you where it is for just a few moments.

As you allow yourself to operate from your deep place of purpose, you enjoy the sense of new opportunities opening up for you. Your energy flows naturally feeling warm and light through your body. You ignite other people's lives and bring surprises and delights for them, increasing your contribution. You create more peak experiences.

You listen at a deeper level with curiosity to hear what is going on for other people and allow them to support your growth. You cut the monkey mind noise in your head that fantasises about what may be going awry and which dilutes your energy.

There's a stillness which brings with it a different quality of being as you travel. There may still be hubbub, distractions and hassle around you and yet you can detach yourself and feel cocooned from it. In this safe and free world, you let go of what's no longer important, quit trying to control everything and instead observe it peacefully without judgment.

Conversations that have been difficult to have can now happen easily. You step back to take decisions based on conscious choice according to your values and your talents rather than having them imposed on you.

You see shapes, patterns and colours in wonderful colours that were dull and grey before. You are happier, healthier and more creative than ever before.

Welcome to an exciting new world.

Love what you do or quit doing it

The person you are today is not the same person you were last month or last year. Today's life experiences are based on what you have created and chosen for yourself along the way, and are instrumental in creating your future. When you wake up and wonder: 'Am I doing what I truly want to be doing? Does this fit with my true sense of purpose?' then you will find it's time to stop, re-evaluate, and reinvent yourself. Perhaps a new career or a different approach to life in general beckons to fire up your passion once more.

Change is a natural process in nature; so, too, it's an essential ingredient in a healthy life. As you become more aware of your purposeful energy you cannot help but change. It may be time for you to ride the escalator to the next level – you may speed up or progress more slowly. You choose the direction and speed. Change can be inconvenient, jolting us out of a comfortable existence, even scary at times. So read on to Chapter 6 to find the bravery needed.

BRAVE ACTION
FOR CHANGE

Take Off the Brakes

Prepare for Resistance

Build a Personal Dream Team

Sharpen your Observation

One Step at a Time

As we listen to other people's stories, we look for parallels in our own lives. We can summon up bravery when we hear how others have trodden a similar path and lived to tell the tale. You may have already made some changes or be facing up to some aspects of your life that you would like to be different. On this final leg of our journey together, we ask, could you be healthier, wealthier, happier in love, find a job that is more stimulating, develop your creative talents or find a way to contribute more in your community or the wider world? What else is possible for you?

Change is an inevitable part of life. If you look back to that slightly younger you of 12 months ago, there will be differences, small or maybe major ones. Life around you does not stand still. The question to ask moving forwards is whether you are an active participant in the change or an unwilling observer.

In *Neuro-linguistic Programming Workbook for Dummies*, I talk about being 'at cause' and being 'at effect'. When you are 'at cause', you don't make excuses. When faced with a challenge, you take responsibility for your destiny as you ask yourself questions like: 'What do I need to do differently?', 'What are the lessons I can learn here?'

When you are 'at effect', you have lost power, you try to justify your actions and blame others. You can't see the way ahead and are likely to be either playing the victim or becoming a passive observer in your life.

It's worth checking in with ourselves regularly to notice if we are taking the 'at cause' route or the 'at effect' one. If you are waiting at home for that perfect partner to drop into your life or the boss to give you the job of your dreams, guess what, you're likely to be waiting for another year! Or what if you wait until you are retired to decide that you never liked your job and didn't do anything about it? Research published in the *Daily Mail* newspaper showed that a third of UK workers coming up for retirement think they made the wrong choice of careers and said they were in work that didn't suit them. A quarter of those surveyed believed that they had stayed in their jobs too long and a tenth regretted going to university and wished they had gone straight into paid employment.

Living a life of 'if only', in which you constantly feel that you have missed the boat, does little for your self-esteem and confidence. If you don't want to live a life full of regrets, it is time to start choosing your own life path. We may need to be thoroughly fed up with the way things are before we make a radical change, or simply meet someone who sparks new ideas for us, but change for the better happens when you do three things differently:

1. Set your intention to focus on what you want to achieve.
2. Pay attention to shifting your energy towards that outcome.
3. Make a personal commitment to embrace change and to ensure that everything you do takes you towards rather than away from your goal.

You may also need a dose of bravery, persistence and help from a support team along the way. As you reflect on the stories in this chapter, notice that change starts in your own hands.

TAKE OFF THE BRAKES

Most of what holds us back from being brave lies inside us – our thoughts and our learned behaviour – rather than in the external world. We behave like animals that have learned to cope with captivity and then never question it.

From NLP trainer, Robert Dilts, I first heard the story of how the Rogue Monkey challenged the status quo in his cage. It goes like this:

> In an experiment in animal behaviour, half a dozen monkeys were put together in a large cage. In the centre of the cage, suspended from the roof, was a bunch of ripe bananas. Below the bananas was a set of steps from which the monkey could pluck the fruit.
>
> However, the steps were wired and connected to a powerful pressure hose. As soon as the steps were touched, jets of cold water sprayed the whole of the cage, drenching all the monkeys. With amazing speed, the monkeys learned that the steps and bananas were out of bounds, and acted collectively to prevent any individual monkey getting too close to them. Social rules were established and enforced.
>
> Once this pattern was established, a monkey was removed from the cage and replaced with a new one. Naturally, the new monkey made straight for the steps. Before he could get close, the rest of the group jump on him, forcibly preventing him from achieving his intention. Very soon, the monkey learned the 'rules' despite having never got wet. And in fact, when the next new

monkey was introduced, it was one of the most ardent in policing the rules.

Over time, all the original monkeys were removed and replaced with new ones. The group taught each new monkey that the steps were off limits. Eventually there were six monkeys in the cage which had never got wet, but which conformed to the rules because 'that's how we've always done it.' The water jets had been long switched off.

Finally, the researchers placed in the cage a bigger, stronger monkey. A rule-breaking monkey. This monkey resists the efforts of the others, breaks with convention, leaps up the steps and gets to eat the bananas. The others watch fearfully, but after a while all of them start to test the steps, and soon they have all changed their behavioural patters. All have bene-fited from the unconventional actions of a single rogue monkey.

(Original source: Robert Dilts. Retold by Nick Owen in *More Magic of Metaphor* and reproduced with permission.)

It's very sobering to stand by people who are frozen to the spot unable to move, scared by the rules, who feel they can't take a step forward or be open to advice; people who've decided it's impossible to change their situation in life. It's also wonderful to see the effect of rogue monkey behaviour.

Too many unhappy people are living life in an artificial comfort zone, rather like driving a car with the handbrake on. It may be safe, but it takes far too much force and effort.

When we question the '*status quo*', we allow new things to happen and are able to break out of the cages we put ourselves in. When we give ourselves permission to really love every part of our lives, then life becomes much more fun.

Thought provokers

» What dream or desire is calling you in your life right now that you are resisting?

» Is there is an area in your life where you are 'playing small'?

» Where is that growing edge, the place that stretches you?

» Consider where you might be standing in your own way and applying the brakes too hard.

» As you read on, begin to focus on all the things that will get better for you as you break the gridlock.

» What risk are you willing to take today?

The other side of the fence

It may be tempting to think that great work sits on 'the other side of the fence' and that the answer to being happy in your work lies simply in jumping out of an organisation and setting up your own business or private practice of some kind. Then life will be wonderful, will it not?

Running a small business or freelance work is not the long-term solution for all, especially in difficult times. For many it can become isolating; you may feel as if you are playing alone in a small and limiting arena. Self-employment can offer more flexible options for working parents, trying to juggle responsibilities; however, there are usually trade-offs in terms of income level and altered status, unless your business is the greater priority than your family. When a business doesn't work out, it takes courage to return to conventional corporate life. Roz has successfully made moves in and out of different types of organisations and proved it's possible to do so. The key is to keep learning and strengthening your ability to get the work you want.

Playing on a bigger stage

When Roz was offered redundancy from her marketing career in a utilities company, she was pleased to get away. She'd lost personal motivation as a series of reorganisations left her with mediocre projects. She joined a smaller creative agency close to home and then freelanced for two years doing marketing for several business owners. Working three days a week in self-employment gave her time that she loved with her young daughter and husband, both of whom had health problems.

However, her workflow was inconsistent and it proved more difficult than she had expected to sell her services. She became acutely aware of the financial insecurity. The commitment to educate her daughter in a private school plus her husband's own unpredictable work weighed heavily on her. A return to corporate life became an attractive option – but this time she needed it to be on her terms.

Initially Roz feared that going back to a corporate job would mean taking a lower level position than she's capable of. However, she reworked her

CV to reframe her experience and focus and to her delight she found that the range of her experience attracted a lot of opportunities.

Although it meant working full time, she found a commercial role where the intellectual challenge was a good match for her. She took the chance to work in a newly-developing market, create her own department and work in a culture where the working patterns were flexible and other opportunities would come up further down the line.

Three years on, she's still there and still learning. 'I love to learn and build my game around real business challenges. There's a bigger stage here for me.'

What Roz particularly enjoys is the opportunity to give back her skills to the younger members of the team. 'I have a lot of experience to pass on, so developing others has proved a real bonus.'

Roz ensures that she keeps evenings and weekends strictly as family time. Her daughter loves the activities on offer at her school and Roz is now finding more time for her own sport and piano playing. Her flexible approach has proved that she can work for others as well as for herself.

PREPARE FOR RESISTANCE

As you make changes in one aspect of your life, other parts of your world change around you too, as James found when he became actively involved in his local community. For a long time he didn't want to pay attention to what was happening on his doorstep, and when he did a new career opened up for him.

Reluctant hero

When you work as a script writer, it's your job to open your audience's eyes to a world they haven't yet discovered or understood. You offer a fresh and engaging perspective, taking them on a journey of discovery following different heroes and heroines.

James' shift in career from script writer to professional coach came about when he became a reluctant hero in his local community. Like many young middle-class professionals living in London in the 1990s, he bought into a less fashionable part of town to provide a home for his new young family. He soon discovered that he'd moved into a street that was alive with villains, drug addicts and prostitutes.

At the same time, the market for his script writing services changed. Instead of writing short, 'perfectly formed' and punchy scripts, he was creating multi-media projects that involved five times the work for the same financial reward. 'I loathed it…my life was not my own,' he says.

Alongside the downturn in his work, James was rebuilding his house and was increasingly disturbed at the escalation of crime in his street. He began to attend local community meetings that he found tedious with no action. 'I was thinking all the time that they were not doing anything.'

The drug situation got worse as a crack house opened right next to his home. Living in fear of walking down the street safely, he felt his life was no longer his own. Feeling pressured by lack of time, low energy levels and hard and unrewarding work, he decided he could no longer live like this which prompted his decision to give the community group a second chance.

This time, instead of expecting 'those people out there' to do something, he took decisive action, by building relationships with the head of the local housing association and volunteering to liaise with the police. It was through this work that he wrote a book called Make It Happen *which was about community action.*

He also came across the profession of coaching. 'I'd never heard there was a job called coaching, and because I had never done it, had no idea that I could make a living out of it.'

There followed a whole new adventure of learning and experimenting with the new career, which in turn led to great assignments that he loved.

Getting actively involved in clearing his local community of drugs was the catalyst for James to improve the quality of his home life and his work. Forming deeper connections with community leaders proved personally transformational. As he discovered: 'Every time you make change out there in the world, it happens for you personally. You change, the outside world changes, it changes you.'

"The secure way is really the insecure way and the way in which the richness of the question accumulates is the right way."

Joseph Campbell

When there's a willingness to take the insecure route, that's where the breakthrough will happen. Because so often from the insecurity comes a new sense of both freedom and control.

James found that having the guts to take a risk opened up a bigger life for himself. If we think about times when you've been sent on the insecure path – pushed out to school by your Mum and Dad, hired or fired into and out of a job, stepped into or out of a relationship, spoken to a stranger, gone alone on a trip, jumped into the sea not knowing the depth. All of these things and more.

When you follow the insecure path, you face your fears and find your real strength in the shadows.

While the strongest resistance usually comes from within us, it's increased when those around us fight against any efforts we put in to challenge the 'status quo.'

Into a new world

When I first met Janet, she was unhappily married, looked exhausted and her self-esteem was at rock bottom. Her husband controlled the bank accounts, did nothing to maintain the house and spent his free time out with his drinking pals. She had no cash to spend on clothes and he seemed to gain a bizarre pleasure from ensuring she stayed at home looking dowdy. He was not physically violent yet he had the power to inflict pain with his snarling comments about her appearance.

She struck me as a very kind, humorous and generous lady. Against his wishes, she plucked up the courage to take herself on a women's 'Return to Work' course to update her office skills. This one step led to a complete change of life. As she gained more skills, she found a part-time administrative job and then a full-time one. Conflict grew at home as her husband fought to manage her earnings and tax allowances, insisting that they were needed for his business.

Over the next three years, she began running as a form of exercise and stress release and started looking after her appearance. A hard worker, Janet put in overtime and secretly saved every spare penny until she could afford to risk divorce and the rental on a new flat for herself and her children. It was a delight to watch Janet blossom into her own natural self as she challenged the relationship with her ex-husband.

Janet told me that she had to hit rock bottom before she heeded her own call to adventure. 'I had married him on the rebound and things gradually got worse without me realising it.' Once she'd made up her mind for change, there was no stopping her. She gained top marks in her IT exams and fought passionately for her financial freedom. Along the way she attracted many strong friends who gave her practical advice and moral support.

When the children left for university, on a whim she packed up her home and goods and set out on an adventure to work in the Middle East. Although that job didn't work out as promised, she met a new man and joined him in his work in Africa. 'It's as if I live in a different world completely. My life today is miles apart from the old one in the UK,' she says.

When you keep quiet and live small, hoping that problems will go away, your self-esteem drops into a downward spiral. These situations take extreme courage to overcome, especially when a number of things need changing at one time: home, relationship, work, money, and health.

BUILD A PERSONAL DREAM TEAM

Change is simpler when you get help. One of those useful mottoes to put on your bathroom mirror is: 'Do only the things that only you can do' and find someone else who can help you with the rest. The most 'successful' people I've met in business all know how to ask for help. They find sponsors, mentors and great assistants. The most content people I've met outside of work don't try to do everything alone. They build a supportive network of friends and family. They recognise the synergy of a group effort.

The idea of a dream team pops up in the world of football where there are various games to build your own fantasy dream team of the top players. A winning sports team is made up of people who specialise in specific skills rather than lots of people who are adequate all-rounders – particularly for skills like goal scoring or tackling. Any team works best by building on the complementary talents of its members.

> ## Top tip
>
> Surround yourself with people who believe in you, sponsor you, mentor and guide you. Find people who want only the best for you and will give their knowledge and support generously in a non-judgemental way; those who will communicate openly and honestly. You want the kind of people with the staying power to support you through the crisis times as well as fair weather. Also find people who are themselves team players, who listen before they act.

Exercise

Selecting your dream team

Now is a good time to consider the people who can help you to tackle your own goals and in so doing enable you to create new possibilities for yourself. Draw up a list of your team candidates in each area.

Physical Energy

Who's going to help you be the fittest, healthiest version of yourself?

Candidates:

....

....

....

....

Tip – look at enlisting professional support from a sports coach or fitness trainer, Yoga or Pilates teacher, nutritionist, doctor or medical consultant.

Mental Energy

Who's going to help you to work with your skills and talents, motivate you to take time out for developing new hobbies and interests and delegate things outside your scope?

Candidates:

....

....

....

....

Tip – find the best teachers or guides for specific skills development or career change, enlist supportive colleagues or managers, workshop leaders, assistants, and business advisers as well as career coaches and headhunters.

Emotional Energy

Who's going to ensure you stay calm and focused when things get tough?

Candidates:

....

....

....

....

Tip – find specialists who can guide you to manage your emotions and hire a personal coach, counsellor or therapist, or meditation teacher. Identify your wisest friends and family members for times of crisis.

Purposeful Energy

Who will enable you to live your core values and connect with your sense of purpose?

Candidates:

....

....

....

....

Tip – look for those who will enable you to see the bigger picture of your life by engaging a professional coach, or finding a spiritual guide.

Once you have drawn up your list of candidates, sit with it awhile. Find out how you feel about these people, logically and intuitively, before you decide who you will work closely with or share your aspirations. A powerful guide will impact on more than one aspect of your energy. Choose who you surround yourself with discernment rather than jumping in.

Quarter-life crisis

'Once you can cope with uncertainty, all kinds of unexpected things happen,' says Nam, who quit her job working for a large charity to set up her own Digital Media business. 'Most of the worrying happened before I took the plunge. Now that I've coped with that, nothing really bothers me.'

A six-month trip to India had sowed the seeds of her long-term dream to establish a children's charity that will be funded by her business. Like many people in their 30s, Nam hit what she calls her 'Quarter-life Crisis' when she needed to find the purpose in her life. She found it in determining to use her web skills to support marginalised groups of young people. 'Once I'd defined my purpose and saw "why" I wanted to change my life, then the details of the "what" and the "how" are following behind.

'I allow myself to be guided by my intuition to do things differently now. I've thrown away the old model of how I worked in a very structured way and what's happened is that I've attracted all kinds of wonderful clients, seemingly without trying.'

Nam's dream team involves several business partners, designers and developers who share a common set of values, as well as a strong family and friends network to come home to. She points to the need for trust in yourself and to have others you trust around you who are willing to share their experience in a supportive way. 'I believe in synchronicity and when I was ready to look and open new doors, all the right people appeared.'

SHARPEN YOUR OBSERVATION

On a day-to-day basis, work is made up of a series of tangible tasks; but in the life context the meaning of work is less tangible. It's about what makes you happy as an individual versus completing the tasks. Open all your senses to become more alert to the way you feel about your work and you will get a sense of whether you are nourished or stifled by your work.

Being busy can become a wonderful indicator of our worth and importance. Yet being busy can block our attention to who we are as people; our powers of observation and aware-ness of self are dulled.

It is valuable to take regular breaks to allow you to step back and watch what is happening in your life. Those with a balanced approach to work will often take a walk round the block during their lunch break to gain perspective. For others, a weekend walk in the woods, a holiday, enforced leave due to illness, extended leave for a sabbatical, or time-out to care for a new baby or older relative may deliver the space needed to think.

Lessons from the working parent

One new mum, Natalie, who runs a team within a bank, told me that she used to think that sabbaticals were a crazy idea until she took maternity leave for the birth of her baby. Natalie shared her personal lessons from her year off:

» *You come back refreshed*

» *You discover you can live on less money*

» *You don't have to judge people by how they spend their holidays – 'I used to go to Bali, and this year in Bognor was also great fun!'*

» *It's OK to find pleasure in the smaller things in life, like watching children play*

» *I am not indispensable*

Having had time to reflect on what was absorbing most of her time and energy, she made changes at work. She now gives her staff more autonomy to make decisions and believes she is a much more effective decision-maker than before. Natalie advocates taking more breaks as a way to gain a clearer perspective on the business. 'Short breaks help me to see where to focus my energy.'

The bank she works for has also gained from her new approach. When others step in to fill her role for a while they build their own skill-set and gain cross-functional experience.

After a few months back at work, Natalie had a newfound confidence to negotiate part-time working hours. She recognises that she's currently delivering the equivalent of a full-time job in part-time hours, thanks to the fact that she's focused on what needs to be done and is also very organised.

'There's still a battle that I need to win as a part-time mum to demonstrate my full commitment to the job.' Part of the battle is to manage the perceptions of others; another is to maintain her inner confidence.

Working parents like Natalie face particular stresses. When managers and employers recognise the contribution they make and find a way to help them, the retention and productivity gains are enormous. According to a survey of working parents by My Family Care in 2009 (www.myfamilycare.co.uk), working parents are getting older and holding more senior positions. Overall they represent around 40 per cent of the workforce, and 94 per cent of them said that when choosing an employer, they look at the level of support for working parents. It's not just about having the right policies in place, but also the attitude of the managers and the way they react on a day-to-day basis.

The survey also highlights the rising number of employees with elder-care issues – people may choose to become working parents but they haven't deliberately chosen to become working carers for their own parents. Members of the 'sandwich generation', who simultaneously care for children and parents, are growing in number. Working professionals are recognising that they will have elder-care responsibilities in the future and are pressing for new support.

As our lives change and the blend of work roles and roles in family life change, we need to check up on our energy levels on a regular basis. This is a life-long exercise to pay attention to what's happening around us so we don't allow ourselves to become overwhelmed by challenges and problems. Remember that Energy Audit in Chapter 1 (see page 23)? Revisit this regularly to ensure that your energy mix is in balance and has not got out of kilter.

Even when things are going well, keep your antennae alert to opportunities that are a better fit for you. Notice your untapped talents and develop new skills and competencies. Listen to what is causing you sleepless nights and anxiety and ask yourself what the message is for you. As you set your intent to get more of what works and less of what doesn't work, then you'll attract new adventures.

Top tip

Check that you are living your values every day. When you are being true to yourself, you will feel healthy, happy and in balance as your energy flows in a sustainable way.

Room with no view

Several of my corporate jobs have taken me to stunning locations but inevitably modern offices are constructed of glass and steel with air conditioning and artificial light. I always experience a huge sense of relief when I leave office buildings. Being outside enables us to regain perspective after the intensity of the workplace and I encourage my clients to take a walk and breaks in fresh air whenever they can.

When Rob shared his tale of life as a European marketing manager it had a familiar ring to it. Travelling for most of the week, Rob would be up at 4 or 5am, travel by taxi to the airport and be off to visit offices all around the world.

As a young man in his 20s, he had found the perks of company travel an exciting bonus. As a senior executive he found that one airport lounge is much like another; one office is much like the next; waking up in a faceless hotel room and not remembering which city you are in soon loses its appeal.

Twenty years of this lifestyle, spending increasing time away from his family, left Rob's energy physically depleted.

Rob enjoyed the mental stimulation of those he met within the organisation and shared the strong corporate values. He met some great people and built very successful programmes. He persevered through the chaos and frustrations of one organisational change after another and began to see that people were being treated as dispensable resources. At its worst, he put up with the strain of 14 new bosses in three years. The complex matrix reporting structure meant he was asked to report to three managers simultaneously, each with different priorities.

'Crunch time came when I worked for several people who I just felt were not holding up the values that were enshrined by the company and ignored the views of experienced employees and customers. We were asking people to do dumb things that made no sense.' Once Rob's values were compromised, he felt compelled to think about leaving.

Today he runs his own consultancy business with a team of enthusiastic associates – his dream team. It's renewed his energy as he feels that he can now work with people whose ethics, morals, values and ways of working he trusts. 'I love working the way we work.'

In making the change, Rob held onto the aspects of his sales career that he loved. He thrives in the business world, developing relationships with customers and leading a team. But he has let go of the heavy baggage that came with an organisation going through badly-managed change. 'I had lost touch with who I was, and now I can see that once more.'

ONE STEP AT A TIME

Other people's stories and other people's lives inevitably set us thinking about our own. As we question what we truly want, we may envy what others have achieved – the beautiful home, the manicured lawn, the strong marriage, the published book, the profitable business, the well-paid job. We need also to recognise the groundwork that has gone into creating that result and what the trade off has been to achieve it. Envying others' success is like wanting an Olympic gold medal without being willing to put in the years of training.

Change involves patience and making tough choices. The first step may be to kill off some habits and behaviours, letting go of activities that we enjoy, to make room for the new. This could be as simple as limiting the time spent surfing the internet after work, or turning off your mobile phone for a few hours every day. Consider enrolling in an Italian evening class instead of nodding off to sleep in front of the TV or having another glass of wine.

In her work on coping with death and dying, Elizabeth Kubler-Ross suggested that people move through a range of stages and reactions in grief: denial, anger, bargaining, depression and acceptance. She found that people go from the initial shock or denial into a period of anxious resistance before accepting a situation and letting go of control. They then start to experiment with new behaviours before making a commitment to a new life. The same principles help us to appreciate the difficulties we face elsewhere in our lives.

Just as we might mourn relationships that have finished, people who've died, friends that we miss, or countries that we've left, letting go can also involve a period of mourning – for opportunities turned down, loss of workmates, time with friends, or ways of working – before experimenting again with new ones.

Recognising that this is happening will provide the impetus to take that first most difficult step, and then the next one and the next. Until the excitement builds of the future.

Flying from one place to the next

Bob flies a glider plane which allows him to travel across the country into the unknown; it's the way he relaxes after work on a summer's evening. Learning to fly was a change he made in his life to give him an engrossing hobby; one that he has pursued steadily for the last ten years. In the air, you can't predict what the weather will do; instead you have to fly from one place to the next.

He says: 'You don't have to take all the decisions at once, nor worry about them. When you fall over, you just pick yourself up.'

As we develop our own goals and plans, we need to be patient taking each stage as it comes. And make sure that we enjoy the view as we go.

The legacy you leave

In Chapter 1, I invited you to write in just a few paragraphs about your life and work as it is today, including a current challenge or possibility for you which has some energy and importance. I now invite you to fast forward to later in your story – say 5, 10 or 20 years from now – to step into the future you are creating.

First you need to find somewhere comfortable to relax. Just close your eyes as you travel into the future, experiencing your future self looking back at you today to tell your own story with detachment, compassion and joy. Imagine that you are walking through a door into the future, meeting the older and wiser version of yourself, perhaps beside a lake, river or sea, or in some other natural place. You are meeting with that future part of you who breathes and smiles easily and can detach readily from the noise and stress of the outside world.

Notice what images come to mind as you greet your older self. Feel the energy flowing through your body. What are you interested in now and how are your talents being put to best use? See how you are spending your time and hear the people around talking about you and the way you love your life. Observe the wise choices you have made, and what you have done to make your relationships with other people so valuable.

As you take it all in, thank your future self for the wisdom and guidance and find your way back to the present moment. Coming back and stretching your body, take three deep breaths and jot down on a piece of paper anything that comes to mind that you want to capture today. Knowing that you can visit your future self is the most powerful resource whenever you need to find the next step on your way.

Ultimately, after listening to everyone else's stories, we are left facing up to our own life's calling and the need to get up and live. Your life is precious and the only one you have.

If you decide to pay attention to every element of your core energy – the sense that calls to you from really deep inside, that you feel is your real self – opportunities will present themselves to you and you will be able to make choices that are congruent with who you really are. As you change yourself, you will influence others around you, leaving the world a better place than when you arrived – just by being who you are.

RESOURCES YOU MAY FIND HELPFUL

PERSONAL COACHING AND WORKSHOPS
WITH THE AUTHOR

As an accredited professional coach, I offer personal coaching by telephone as well as face-to-face coaching and workshops for clients who are committed to living their lives to the full.

Contact me at kate@kateburton.co.uk or via my website www.kateburton.co.uk for details of the 'Live Life. Love Work.' programmes.

BIBLIOGRAPHY

Now that you have read this book, keep reading. Scan the bookshelves for titles that will inspire you to find the kind of work you really want to and the tools and confidence to make change. Here are some that I feel will make a difference on the way.

Building Self-confidence for Dummies, Kate Burton and Brinley Platts, John Wiley & Sons Ltd, 2005

Crossing the Unknown Sea: Work as a Pilgrimage of Identity, David Whyte, Riverhead Books, 2001

Job-Hunting and Career Change All-in-One for Dummies, Rob Yeung, John Wiley & Sons Ltd, 2007

More Magic of Metaphor: Stories for Leaders, Influencers and Motivators and Spiral Dynamics Wizards, Nick Owen, Crown House Publishing, 2004

Neuro-Linguistic Programming for Dummies, Romilla Ready and Kate Burton, John Wiley & Sons Ltd, 2004

Neuro-Linguistic Programming Workbook for Dummies, Romilla Ready and Kate Burton, John Wiley & Sons Ltd, 2008

The Dark Side of the Light Chasers: Reclaiming Your Power, Creativity, Brilliance and Dreams, Debbie Ford, Hodder & Stoughton, 2001

The Dance of Connection: How to Talk to Someone When You're Mad, Hurt, Scared, Frustrated, Insulted, Betrayed, or Desperate, Harriet Goldhor Lerner, Quill, 2002

The Definitive Job Book: Rules from the Recruitment Insiders, Anne Watson, Capstone Publishing, 2007

The Places That Scare You: A Guide to Fearlessness, Pema Chodron, Harper Collins, 2004

The Power of Story: Change Your Story, Change Your Destiny in Business and in Life, Jim Loehr, Free Press, 2008

The Soul of Money: Reclaiming the Wealth of Our Inner Resources, Lynne Twist, W.W.Norton & Co, 2006

When Work Doesn't Work Anymore, Elizabeth Perle McKenna, SOS Free Stock, 1997

Yoga and the Search for the True Self, Stephen Cope, Bantam Books, 2001

USEFUL WEBSITES

To find an accredited coach in your area, check out the International Coaching Federation at www.coachfederation. org.

To find a skilled therapist for long-term, one-to-one work, see the UK Council for Psychotherapy at www.ukcp.org.uk or the British Association for Counselling and Psychotherapy at www.bacp.co.uk.

To find a qualified nutritionist, contact the Institute of Optimum Nutrition at www.ion.ac.uk.

INDEX